Careers in Focus

RETAIL

Third Edition

W.J. KEENAN MEDIA CENTER

Ferguson

An imprint of Infobase Publishing

Ferguson
An imprint of Infobase Publishing
132 West 31st Street
New York NY 10001

Library of Congress Cataloging-in-Publication Data

Careers in focus. Retail. — 3rd ed.
    p. cm.
  Includes index.
  ISBN-13: 978-0-8160-6593-6 (hc : alk. paper) 1. Retail trade—Vocational guidance—Juvenile literature. 2. Selling—Vocational guidance—Juvenile literature. 3. Sales personnel—Job descriptions—Juvenile literature. I. Title: Retail.
  HF5429.29.C37 2007
  381'.102373—dc22   2006036343

Ferguson books are available at special discounts when purchased in bulk quantities for businesses, associations, institutions, or sales promotions. Please call our Special Sales Department in New York at (212) 967-8800 or (800) 322-8755.

You can find Ferguson on the World Wide Web at http://www.fergpubco.com

Text design by David Strelecky
Cover design by Salvatore Luongo

Printed in the United States of America

MP Hermitage 10 9 8 7 6 5 4 3 2 1

This book is printed on acid-free paper.

Table of Contents

Introduction

Although shopping in a retail store, from a catalog, or from the Internet is a common activity, the actual work of a retail organization is a mystery to most people. One of the primary tasks of retail stores is to be constantly aware of the changing lifestyle habits, needs, and desires of their customers. They must anticipate customers' wishes days, weeks, and even months ahead of time. In addition, because of their competition, retailers must race to get the merchandise first, to offer the best service, and to provide the most attractive setting so that customers will be eager to shop in their particular establishment.

In general, stores can be divided into two major groups: specialty stores and general merchandise stores. Specialty stores carry just one category of merchandise or several types of closely related merchandise. Specialty stores include apparel shops, building supply stores, automobile dealers, gas stations, household appliance stores, florists, optical goods stores, news stands, drugstores, shoe stores, sporting goods stores, computer sales outlets, grocery stores, and supermarkets.

General merchandise stores include variety stores, junior department stores, and department stores. They stock a multitude of different items under one roof. Variety stores carry broad assortments of goods at limited prices. Junior department stores carry various categories of merchandise in somewhat broader price ranges. Department stores carry large assortments of apparel, home goods, and staple items in even more extensive price ranges. When specialty stores or general merchandise stores feature self-service and bargain prices, they usually are called mass merchandisers.

Some stores have only a single location, while others, such as chain organizations and franchise operations, have more than one. The largest stores have several thousand locations. Chain organizations are parent stores with branches. Franchise operations allow individually owned stores to market or sell their line of goods.

The major functions of retailing may be divided into five categories: merchandising and buying; store operations; sales promotion; bookkeeping/accounting; and personnel. *Merchandising and buying* determines the assortment and amount of merchandise to be sold. *Store operations* maintains the retailer's building. *Sales promotion and advertising* informs customers and potential customers about available goods and services. *Bookkeeping and accounting workers* are charged with the task of keeping records of money spent and received, as well as records of payrolls, taxes, and money due from customers. *The personnel department* staffs the store with qualified people.

Many people are involved in buying merchandise in large organizations, whereas in small stores one or two persons may do all the buying. Before merchandise can be purchased, however, *store executives* must plan for the kinds and amounts of merchandise to be bought. Analyses of previous sales reveal how successful the store was in selling similar merchandise during a comparable period. After these records are examined and the amount of such merchandise already in the store is determined, an executive decides on the amount of new merchandise to be purchased. The person who does this kind of planning and supervising in a large organization may be called a *merchandiser* or *merchandise manager.*

After the general buying plan has been established, the *buyer* must go to manufacturers' showrooms or to factories in the United States or abroad to look at the merchandise and select from the available items that will be in demand for the coming season. Contracts then are signed for the delivery of the goods. Buying may be completed as much as six months before the buyer anticipates selling the goods in the store.

Store managers of chain stores and *department managers* in branch stores are responsible not only for merchandise but also for department or store operation. The department manager acts as a departmental supervisor for the buyer in the branch store but does not have the responsibility for the actual selection and purchase of merchandise.

In a small store, usually one store manager has final responsibility for all operational activities. In a larger organization, each function may be supervised by a separate manager. Managers could be in charge of receiving goods, marking them, placing them in the stockrooms or warehouse, and subsequently moving the goods to the selling floor. After the merchandise is sold, other managers may be in charge of wrapping stations and delivery services. Supervision of the selling floor and handling of customer returns and complaints also are activities carried out by operating personnel. Elevator service, housekeeping service, and the relocation of goods for special selling seasons are further responsibilities of operating personnel.

Many large retail organizations maintain sales promotion, advertising, and display staffs. The people who work in these fields are responsible for the overall impression that the store creates. A favorable image generates more business for the retailer. Those who produce advertising include the *advertising manager, copywriters, artists, photographers*, and *typographers*.

Most of the positions in marketing require creative talent; therefore, those who apply for these jobs usually excel in writing or artwork, or they have had experience in staging shows or running school publicity events.

In small stores, most owners or managers employ part-time *accountants* to take care of the financial records of the firm. The finances of a large store or chain of stores usually are administered by a *controller*, who has an accounting background and knowledge of computer systems.

Retailing in today's economy demands both knowledge of the field and management ability. More competition, better-educated customers, and more diversified types of retailing allow for fewer errors, especially on the part of small firm owners. Additional challenges for U.S. retailers are the country's maturing population, its rapidly changing culture, an influx of people from other countries, and a growth in technology, all of which provide a more dynamic and less predictable market. Because retailing is still primarily a business of people working with and serving other people, the use of computerized systems for record keeping, merchandise-handling mechanization, and automatic vending machines has not displaced many sales workers.

The Internet is now changing the way that mass retailers do business, and it will continue to have a huge impact in the future. The benefit of selling on the Internet for retailers is the ability to reach new customers, both domestic and foreign, and at a much lower cost. Consumers have the convenience of shopping from home or office for groceries, clothes, or insurance, as well as planning a vacation.

Each article in *Careers in Focus: Retail* discusses a particular retail-related career in detail. The articles appear in Ferguson's *Encyclopedia of Careers and Vocational Guidance* but have been updated and revised with the latest information from the U.S. Department of Labor, professional organizations, and other sources. The following paragraphs detail the sections and features that appear in the book.

The **Quick Facts** section provides a brief summary of the career, including recommended school subjects, personal skills, work environment, minimum educational requirements, salary ranges, certification or licensing requirements, and employment outlook. This section also provides acronyms and identification numbers for the following government classification indexes: the Dictionary of

Occupational Titles (DOT), the Guide to Occupational Exploration (GOE), the National Occupational Classification (NOC) Index, and the Occupational Information Network (O*NET)-Standard Occupational Classification System (SOC) index. The DOT, GOE, and O*NET-SOC indexes have been created by the U.S. government; the NOC index is Canada's career classification system. Readers can use the identification numbers listed in the Quick Facts section to access further information about a career. Print editions of the DOT (*Dictionary of Occupational Titles*. Indianapolis, Ind.: JIST Works, 1991) and GOE (*The Complete Guide for Occupational Exploration*. Indianapolis, Ind.: JIST Works, 1993) are available at libraries. Electronic versions of the NOC (http://www23.hrdc-drhc.gc.ca) and O*NET-SOC (http://online.onetcenter.org) are available on the Internet. When no DOT, GOE, NOC, or O*NET-SOC numbers are present, this means that the U.S. Department of Labor or Human Resources Development Canada has not created a numerical designation for this career. In this instance, you will see the acronym "N/A" or not available.

The **Overview** section is a brief introductory description of the duties and responsibilities involved in this career. Oftentimes, a career may have a variety of job titles. When this is the case, alternative career titles are presented. The **History** section describes the history of the particular job as it relates to the overall development of its industry or field. **The Job** describes the primary and secondary duties of the job. **Requirements** discusses high school and postsecondary education and training requirements, any certification or licensing that is necessary, and other personal requirements for success in the job. **Exploring** offers suggestions on how to gain experience in or knowledge of the particular job before making a firm educational and financial commitment. The focus is on what can be done while still in high school (or in the early years of college) to gain a better understanding of the job. The **Employers** section gives an overview of typical places of employment for the job. **Starting Out** discusses the best ways to land that first job, be it through the college placement office, newspaper ads, or personal contact. The **Advancement** section describes what kind of career path to expect from the job and how to get there. **Earnings** lists salary ranges and describes the typical fringe benefits. The **Work Environment** section describes the typical surroundings and conditions of employment— whether indoors or outdoors, noisy or quiet, social or independent. Also discussed are typical hours worked, any seasonal fluctuations, and the stresses and strains of the job. The **Outlook** section summarizes the job in terms of the general economy and industry projections. For the most part, Outlook information is obtained from the U.S. Bureau of Labor Statistics and is supplemented by information taken from professional associations. Job growth terms follow those used in the *Occupational Outlook Handbook*. Growth described as "much faster than the average" means an increase of 27 percent or more. Growth described as "faster than the average" means an increase of 18 to 26 percent. Growth described as "about as fast as the average" means an increase of 9 to 17 percent. Growth described as "more slowly than the average" means an increase of 0 to 8 percent. "Decline" means a decrease by any amount. Each article ends with **For More Information,** which lists organizations that provide information on training, education, internships, scholarships, and job placement.

Careers in Focus: Retail also includes photographs, informative sidebars, and interviews with professionals in the field.

Antiques and Art Dealers

QUICK FACTS

School Subjects
Art
Art History
Business
Family and consumer science

Personal Skills
Artistic
Leadership/management

Work Environment
Primarily indoors
Primarily multiple locations

Minimum Education Level
High school diploma

Salary Range
$15,000 to $30,000 to
$1,000,000+

Certification or Licensing
None available

Outlook
About as fast as the average

DOT
N/A

GOE
N/A

NOC
0621

O*NET-SOC
N/A

OVERVIEW

Antiques and art dealers make a living acquiring, displaying, and selling antiques and art. By strict definition, antiques are often defined as items more than 100 years old. However, over the last two decades, the term "antique" has been applied to furniture, jewelry, clothing, art, household goods, and many other collectibles, dating back to as recently as the 1970s. People collect a wide array of items, from traditional paintings and sculptures to unique period toys and cigar boxes. Many antiques and art dealers are self-employed and go into business after discovering an interest in collecting pieces themselves. The Antiques and Collectibles Dealer Association estimates that there are approximately 200,000 to 250,000 antique dealers in the United States, based in antique shops, antique malls, and on the Internet.

HISTORY

Interest in collecting antiques and art can be traced to the Renaissance, when people began to admire and prize Greek and Roman antiquities such as coins, manuscripts, sculptures, paintings, and pieces of architecture. In order to fulfill public interest and curiosity, as well as to supply the growing number of private and public collections, many pieces from Egypt, Italy, and Greece were looted and carried off to other countries.

The collectibles market, as it is known today, consists of everyday household objects, as well as furniture, clothing, art, and even automobiles, usually originating from another time period. After World War I, interest in collectibles grew. Many people began to purchase, preserve, and display pieces in their homes. As interest grew, so did the need for antiques and art businesses and dealers.

There are different categories of collectibles and different ways and reasons to acquire them. Some people choose to collect pieces from different time periods such as American Colonial or Victorian; others collect by the pattern or brand, such as Chippendale furniture or Coca-Cola memorabilia. Some people collect objects related to their career or business. For example, a physician may collect early surgical instruments, while a pharmacist may be interested in antique apothecary cabinets. A growing category in the collectibles industry is ephemera, which includes theater programs, postcards, cigarette cards, and food labels, among others. These items were produced without lasting value or survival in mind. Though many pieces of ephemera can be purchased inexpensively, others, especially items among the first of their kind or in excellent condition, are rare and considered very valuable.

Some larger antiques and art dealers specialize and deal only with items from a particular time period or design. Most, however, collect, buy, and sell most previously owned household items and decor. Such shops will carry items ranging from dining room furniture to jewelry to cooking molds.

The standard of what is worth collecting constantly changes with time and the public's tastes and interests. Art tastes range from traditional to contemporary, from Picasso to Warhol. Items representing the rock music industry of the 1960s and 1970s, as well as household items and furniture of the 1970s, are highly sought after today. Dealers not only stock their stores with items currently in demand but keep an eye on the collectibles of the future.

THE JOB

For Sandra Naujokas, proprietor of Favorite Things Antique Shop, in Orland Park, Illinois, the antiques business is never boring. Over 25 years ago, she started a collection of English-style china, and she's been hooked on antiques and collecting ever since. Naujokas spends her workday greeting customers and answering any questions they may have. When business slows down, she cleans the store and prices inventory. Sometimes people will bring in items for resale. It's up to Naujokas to carefully inspect each piece and settle on a price. She relies on pricing manuals such as *Kovels' Antiques & Collectibles Price List* and *Schroeder's Antiques Price Guide,* which give guidelines and suggested prices on a wide range of items.

Naujokas also goes on a number of shopping expeditions each year to restock her store. Besides rummage sales and auctions, she relies on buying trips to different parts of the country and abroad to find regional items. At times, she is invited to a person's home to view items for sale. "It's important to be open to all possibilities," Naujokas says.

She also participates in several shows a year, in order to reach customers that normally would not travel to the store's location. "You need to do a variety of things to advertise your wares," Naujokas advises.

She also promotes her business by advertising in her town's travel brochure, the local newspapers, and by direct mail campaigns. Her schedule is grueling, as the store is open seven days a week, but Naujokas enjoys the work and the challenge of being an antique dealer. Besides the social aspect—interacting with all sorts of people and situations—Naujokas loves having the first choice of items for her personal collections. Her advice for people interested in having their own antique store? "You have to really like the items you intend to sell."

REQUIREMENTS

High School

You can become an antique or art dealer with a high school diploma, though many successful dealers have become specialists in their field partly through further education. While in high school, concentrate on history and art classes to familiarize yourself with the particular significance and details of different periods in time and the corresponding art of the period. Consider studying home economics if you plan to specialize in household items. This knowledge can come in handy when distinguishing a wooden rolling pin from a wooden butter paddle, for example.

Taking English and speech classes to improve communication skills is also helpful. Antiques and art dealing is a people-oriented business. For this reason, it's crucial to be able to deal efficiently with different types of people and situations. Operating your own small business will also require skills such as accounting, simple bookkeeping, and marketing, so business classes are recommended.

Postsecondary Training

While a college education is not required, a degree in fine arts, art history, or history will give you a working knowledge of the antiques you sell and the historical periods from which they originated.

Another option is obtaining a degree in business or entrepreneurship. Such knowledge will help you to run a successful business.

Certification or Licensing

Presently, there are no certification programs available for antique dealers. However, if you plan to open your own antique store, you will need a local business license or permit.

In addition, if you wish to conduct appraisals, it will be necessary to take appraisal courses that are appropriate for your interest or antique specialty. Certification is not required of those interested in working as an appraiser, but it is highly recommended, according to the International Society of Appraisers—which administers an accreditation and certification program to its members. Obtaining accreditation or certification will demonstrate your knowledge and expertise in appraisal and attract customers. To obtain accreditation, candidates must have three years of experience in appraising, complete the ISA Core Course in Appraisal Studies, and pass an examination. In order to become certified, individuals must complete additional training in their specialty area, submit two appraisals for peer review, complete professional development study, and pass a comprehensive examination.

Other Requirements

To be an antique or art dealer, you'll need patience—and lots of it. Keeping your store well stocked with antiques, art, or other collectibles takes numerous buying trips to auctions, estate sales, flea markets, rummage sales, and even foreign countries. Many times you'll have to sort through boxes of ordinary "stuff" before coming across a treasure. Unless you're lucky enough to have a large staff, you will have to make these outings by yourself. However, most dealers go into the profession because they enjoy the challenge of hunting for valuable pieces.

Tact is another must-have quality for success in this industry. Remember the old adage—one person's trash is another person's treasure.

Finally, with the growth of online auction sites such as eBay, computer skills have come to be an essential part of the antique or collectible dealer's toolkit.

EXPLORING

If you want to explore this field further, you may want to start by visiting an antique store or art gallery. If you see valuable treasures as opposed to dull paintings, old furniture, outdated books, or dusty collectibles, chances are this is the job for you.

You can also tune to an episode of public television's traveling antique show, *Antiques Roadshow*. The premise? Locals are encouraged to bring family treasures or rummage sale bargains for appraisal by antique industry experts.

EMPLOYERS

Many antiques and art dealers are self-employed, operating their own shops or renting space at a local mall. Others operate solely through traveling art shows or through mail-order catalogues. Some dealers prefer to work as employees of larger antique or art galleries. In general, the more well known the dealer, the more permanent and steady the business. Prestigious auction houses such as Christie's or Sotheby's are attractive places to work, but competition for such jobs is fierce.

STARTING OUT

All dealers have a great interest in antiques or art and are collectors themselves. Often, their businesses result from an overabundance of their personal collections. There are many ways to build your collection and create inventory worthy of an antique business. Attending yard sales is an inexpensive way to build your inventory; you'll never know what kind of valuables you will come across. Flea markets, local art galleries, and antique malls will provide great purchasing opportunities and give you the chance to check out the competition. Sandra Naujokas finds that spring is an especially busy time for collecting. As people do their "spring cleaning," many decide to part with household items and décor they no longer want or need.

ADVANCEMENT

For those working out of their homes or renting showcase space at malls or larger shops, advancement in this field can mean opening your own antique shop or art gallery. Besides a business license, dealers who open their own stores need to apply for a seller's permit and a state tax identification number.

At this point, advancement is based on the success of the business. To ensure that their business thrives and expands, dealers need to develop advertising and marketing ideas to keep their business in the public's eye. Besides using the local library or Internet for ideas on opening their own businesses, newer dealers often turn to people who are already in the antiques and art business for valuable advice.

EARNINGS

It is difficult to gauge what antiques and art dealers earn, because of the vastness of the industry. Some internationally known, high-end antique stores and art galleries dealing with many pieces of priceless furniture or works of art may make millions of dollars in yearly profits. This, however, is the exception. It is impractical to compare the high-end dealer with the lower-end market. The majority of antiques and art dealers are comparatively small in type of inventory. Some dealers work only part time or rent showcase space from established shops.

According to a survey conducted by the Antiques and Collectibles Dealer Association, the average showcase dealer earns about $1,000 a month in gross profits. From there, each dealer earns a net profit as determined by the piece or pieces sold, after overhead and other business costs. Note that annual earnings vary greatly for antiques and art dealers due to factors such as the size and specialization of the store, location, the market, and current trends and tastes of the public.

WORK ENVIRONMENT

Much of antiques and art dealers' time is spent indoors. Many smaller antique shops and art galleries do not operate with a large staff, so dealers must be prepared to work alone at times. Also, there may be large gaps of time between customers. Most stores are open at least five days a week and operate during regular business hours, though some have extended shopping hours in the evening.

However, dealers are not always stuck in their store. Buying trips and shopping expeditions give them opportunities to restock their inventory, not to mention explore different regions of the country or world. Sandra Naujokas finds that spring is the busiest time for building her store's merchandise, while the holiday season is a busy selling time.

OUTLOOK

According to the Antiques and Collectibles Dealer Association (ACDA), the collectibles industry should enjoy moderate growth in future years. The Internet has quickly become a popular way to buy and sell antiques and art. Though this medium has introduced collecting to many people worldwide, it has also had an adverse affect on the industry, namely for dealers and businesses that sell antiques and art in more traditional settings such as a shop or mall or at a trade show. However, Jim Tucker, co-founder and director of the ACDA, predicts that the popularity of Web sites devoted to selling collectibles will level off. There is a great social aspect to collecting art and antiques. Tucker feels that people want to see, feel, and touch the items they are interested in purchasing, which is obviously not possible to do while surfing the Web.

Though the number of authentic antique art and collectibles—items more than 100 years old—is limited, new items will be in vogue as collectibles. Also, people will be ready to sell old furniture and other belongings to make room for new, modern purchases. It is unlikely that there will ever be a shortage of inventory worthy of an antique shop or art gallery.

FOR MORE INFORMATION

For industry information, antique show schedules, and appraisal information, contact
  Antique and Collectible Associations
  PO Box 4389
  Davidson, NC 28036-4389
  Tel: 800-287-7127
  Email: info@antiqueandcollectible.com
  http://www.antiqueandcollectible.com

For art resources and listings of galleries, contact
  Art Dealers Association of America
  575 Madison Avenue
  New York, NY 10022-2511
  Tel: 212-940-8590
  Email: adaa@artdealers.org
  http://www.artdealers.org

Contact the FADA for information on art galleries nationwide and special events.
  Fine Art Dealers Association (**FADA**)
  PO Box D1
  Carmel, CA 93921-0729
  http://www.fada.com

For information about appraising and certification, contact
International Society of Appraisers
1131 Seventh Street SW, Suite 105
Renton, WA 98057-1215
Tel: 206-241-0359
Email: isahq@isa-appraisers.org
http://www.isa-appraisers.org

For programming schedules and tour information on the public television show that highlights unique and sometimes priceless antique finds, visit
Antiques Roadshow
http://www.pbs.org/wgbh/pages/roadshow

For information on collecting, art and antique shows, and collecting clubs, visit
Collectors.org
http://www.collectors.org

Automobile Sales Workers

QUICK FACTS

School Subjects
Business
Speech

Personal Skills
Communication/ideas
Helping/teaching

Work Environment
Primarily indoors
Primarily one location

Minimum Education Level
High school diploma

Salary Range
$20,000 to $38,688 to
$75,000+

Certification or Licensing
Voluntary

Outlook
About as fast as the average

DOT
273

GOE
08.02.01

NOC
6421

O*NET-SOC
11-2022.00

OVERVIEW

Automobile sales workers inform customers about new or used automobiles, and they prepare payment, financing, and insurance papers for customers who have purchased a vehicle. It is their job to persuade the customer that the product they are selling is the best choice. They prospect new customers by mail, by telephone, or through personal contacts. To stay informed about their products, sales workers regularly attend training sessions about the vehicles they sell. There are approximately 269,000 automobile sales workers employed in the United States.

HISTORY

By the 1920s, nearly 20,000 automobile dealerships dotted the American landscape as the "Big Three" automobile makers—Ford, General Motors, and Chrysler—increased production every year to meet the public's growing demand for automobiles. Automobile sales workers began to earn higher and higher wages. As automobiles became more popular, the need for an organization to represent the growing industry became evident. In 1917, the National Automobile Dealers Association (NADA) was founded to change the way Congress viewed automobiles. In the early years, NADA worked to convince Congress that cars weren't luxuries, as they had been classified, but vital to the economy. The group prevented the government from converting all automotive factories to wartime work facilities during World War I and reduced a proposed luxury tax on automobiles from five percent to three percent.

During the lean years of the Depression in the early 1930s, automobile sales fell sharply until President Franklin Delano Roosevelt's New Deal helped jumpstart the industry. Roosevelt signed the Code of Fair Competition for the Motor Vehicle Retailing Trade, which established standards in the automotive manufacturing and sales industries. By 1942, the number of dealerships in the United States more than doubled to 44,000.

Automobile sales workers have suffered an image problem for much of the career's history. Customers sometimes felt that they were pressured to purchase new cars at unfair prices and that the dealer's profit was too large. The 1958 Price Labeling Law, which mandated cars display window stickers listing manufacturer suggested retail prices and other information, helped ease relations between sales workers and their customers. However, in the fiercely competitive automobile market, sales workers' selling methods and the thrifty customer remained at odds.

When it came to used vehicles, there was no way for customers to know whether they were getting a fair deal. Even in the automobile's early history, used vehicles were popular. From 1919 through the 1950s, used car sales consistently exceeded new car sales. Despite the popularity of used vehicles, the automobile sales industry didn't quite know how to handle them. Some dealers lost money on trade-ins when they stayed on the lot too long. After debating for years how to handle trade-ins, dealers finally began today's common practice of applying their value toward down payments on new cars.

The industry suffered personnel shortages when the armed forces recruited mechanics during World War II. This affected the service departments of dealerships, which traditionally have generated the biggest profits, and many dealers had to be creative to stay in business. During these lean times, sales gimmicks such as giveaways and contests came into increased use. According to a history of NADA, one Indiana dealer bought radios, refrigerators, freezers, and furnaces to sell in his showroom and sold toys at Christmas to stay in business.

The energy crisis of the 1970s brought hard times to the entire automotive industry. Many dealerships were forced to close, and those that survived made little profit. In 1979 alone, 600 dealerships closed. As of 2006, according to the NADA, there were 21,495 dealerships nationwide (down from 47,500 in 1951), accounting for about 20 percent of all retail sales and employing more than 1.1

million people. Most dealerships today sell more makes of cars than dealerships of the past. Still, they face competition from newer forms of automobile retailers, such as automotive superstores, the automotive equivalent to discount stores like Wal-Mart. Also, automotive information is becoming more widely available on the Internet, eroding the consumer's need for automobile sales workers as a source of information about automobiles.

THE JOB

The automobile sales worker's main task is to sell. Today, many dealerships try to soften the image of the salesperson by emphasizing no pressure, even one-price shopping. But automobile dealers expect their employees to sell, and selling in most cases involves some degree of persuasion. The automobile sales worker informs customers of everything there is to know about a particular vehicle. A good sales worker finds out what the customer wants or needs and suggests automobiles that may fit that need—empowering the customer with choice and a feeling that he or she is getting a fair deal.

Since the sticker price on new cars is only a starting point to be bargained down, and since many customers come to dealerships already knowing which car they would like to buy, sales workers spend much of their time negotiating the final selling price.

Most dealerships have special sales forces for new cars, used cars, trucks, recreational vehicles, and leasing operations. In each specialty, sales workers learn all aspects of the product they must sell. They may attend information and training seminars sponsored by manufacturers. New car sales workers, especially, are constantly learning new car features. Sales workers inform customers about a car's performance, fuel economy, safety features, and luxuries or accessories. They are able to talk about innovations over previous models, engine and mechanical specifications, ease of handling, and ergonomic designs. Good sales workers also keep track of competing models' features.

In many ways, used car sales workers have a more daunting mass of information to keep track of. Whereas new car sales workers concentrate on the most current features of an automobile, used car sales workers must keep track of all features from several model years. Good used car dealers can look at a car and note immediately the make, model, and year of a car. Because of popular two- and three-year leasing options, the used car market has increased by nearly 50 percent in the last 10 years.

Successful sales workers are generally good readers of a person's character. They can determine exactly what it is a customer is looking for in a new car. They must be friendly and understanding of customers' needs in order to put them at ease (due to the amount of money involved, car buying is an unpleasant task for most people). They are careful not to oversell the car by providing the customers with information they may not care about or understand, thus confusing them. For example, if a customer cares only about style, sales workers will not impress upon him all of the wonderful intricacies of a new high-tech engine design.

Sales workers greet customers and ask if they have any questions about a particular model. It's very important for sales workers to have immediate and confident answers to all questions about the vehicles they're selling. When a sale is difficult, they occasionally use psychological methods, or subtle "prodding," to influence customers. Some sales workers use aggressive selling methods and pressure the customer to purchase the car. Although recent trends are turning away from the pressure-sell, competition will keep these types of selling methods prevalent in the industry, albeit at a slightly toned-down level.

Customers usually make more than one visit to a dealership before purchasing a new or used car. Because one sales worker "works" the customer on the first visit—forming an acquaintanceship and learning the customer's personality—he or she will usually stay with that customer until the sale is made or lost. The sales worker usually schedules times for the customer to come in and talk more about the car in order to stay with the customer through the process and not lose the sale to another sales worker. Sales workers may make follow-up phone calls to make special offers or remind customers of certain features that make a particular model better than that of the competition, or they may send mailings for the same purpose.

In addition to providing the customer with information about the car, sales workers discuss financing packages, leasing options, and warranty. When the sale is made, they go over the contract with the customer and obtain a signature. Frequently, the exact model with all of the features the customer requested is not in the dealership, and the sales worker must place an order with the manufacturer or distributor. When purchasing a new or used vehicle, many customers trade in their old vehicle. Sales workers appraise the trade-in and offer a price.

At some dealerships, sales workers also do public relations and marketing work. They establish promotions to get customers into their showrooms, print fliers to distribute in the local community,

An automobile sales worker discusses the purchase of an SUV with a family. *(Frank Siteman, Index Stock Imagery)*

and make television advertisements. In order to keep their name in the back (or front) of the customer's mind, they may send former customers birthday and holiday cards or similar "courtesies." Most of the larger dealerships also have an auto maintenance and repair service department. Sales workers may help customers establish a periodic maintenance schedule or suggest repair work.

Computers are used at a growing number of dealerships. Customers use computers to answer questions they may have, consult price indexes, check on the availability of parts, and even compare the car they're interested in with the competition's equivalent. Although computers can't replace human interaction and sell the car to customers who need reassurances, they do help the customer feel more informed and more in control when buying a car.

REQUIREMENTS

High School

Because thorough knowledge of automobiles—from how they work to how they drive and how they are manufactured—is essential for a successful sales worker, automotive maintenance classes in high school are an excellent place to begin. Classes in English, speech, drama, and psychology will help you to achieve the excellent speaking skills you will need to make a good sale and gain customer confidence and respect. Classes in business and mathematics will teach you to manage and prioritize your work load, prepare goals, and work confidently with customer financing packages. As computers become increasingly prevalent in every aspect of the industry, you should take as many computer classes as you can. Speaking a second language will give you an advantage, especially in major cities with large minority populations.

Postsecondary Training

Those who seek management-level positions will have a distinct advantage if they possess a college degree, preferably in business or marketing, but other degrees, whether in English, economics, or psychology, are no less important, so long as applicants have good management skills and can sell cars. Many schools offer degrees in automotive marketing and automotive aftermarket management that prepare students to take high-level management positions. Even with a two- or four-year degree in hand, many dealerships may not begin new hires directly as managers but start them out as sales workers.

Certification or Licensing

By completing the certified automotive merchandiser (CAM) program offered by the NADA, students seeking entry-level positions gain a significant advantage. Certification assures employers that workers have the basic skills they require.

Other Requirements

In today's competitive job market you will need a high school diploma to land a job that offers growth possibilities, a good salary, and challenges; this includes jobs in the automobile sales industry. Employers prefer to hire entry-level employees who have had some experience in automotive services or in retail sales. They look for candidates who have good verbal, business, mathematics, electronics, and computer skills. A number of automotive sales and services courses and degrees are offered today at community colleges, vocational schools, independent organizations, and manufacturers. Sales workers should possess a valid driver's license and have a good driving record.

Sales workers must be enthusiastic, well-organized self-starters who thrive in a competitive environment. They must show excitement and authority regarding each type of car they sell and convince customers, without being too pushy (though some pressure on the customer usually helps make the sale), that the car they're interested in is the "right" car, at the fairest price. Sales workers must be able to read a customer's personality and know when to be outgoing and when to pull back and be more reserved. A neat, professional appearance is also very important for sales workers.

EXPLORING

Automobile trade magazines and books, in addition to selling-technique and business books, are excellent sources of information for someone considering a career in this field. Local and state automobile and truck dealer associations can also provide you with information on career possibilities in automobile and truck sales. Your local Yellow Pages has a listing under "associations" for dealer organizations in your area.

Students interested in automobile sales work might first stop by their local dealer and ask about training programs and job requirements there. On a busy day at any dealership, several sales workers will be on the floor selling cars. Students can witness the basic selling process by going to dealerships and unobtrusively watching and listening as sales workers talk with customers. Many dealerships hire students part time to wash and clean cars. This is a good way to see the types of challenges and pressures automobile sales workers experience every day. Although it may take a special kind of sales skill or a different approach to sell a $30,000 vehicle over $50 shoes, any type of retail sales job that requires frequent interaction

Facts About the Automotive Sales Industry

- There were 21,495 new car dealerships in the United States in 2006.

- California (1,659), Texas (1,369), Pennsylvania (1,227), New York (1,190), and Illinois (1,000) had the highest number of dealerships.

- More than 231,000 new- and used-vehicle salespeople are employed in the United States.

- In 2005, more than 238 million vehicles were in operation in the United States.

Source: National Automobile Dealers Association

with customers will prepare students for work as an automobile sales worker.

EMPLOYERS

Franchised automobile dealerships employ the majority of automobile sales workers in the United States. A franchised automobile dealer is formally recognized and authorized by the manufacturer to sell its vehicles. A small number of sales workers are employed by used car dealerships that are strictly independent and not recognized by any manufacturer. Automotive superstores need automobile sales workers as well, although some may argue that these workers aren't truly automobile sales specialists, because they tend to have less training and experience in the automotive area.

STARTING OUT

Generally, those just out of high school are not going to land a job as an automobile sales worker; older customers do not feel comfortable making such a large investment through a teenager. Employers prefer to see some automotive service experience with certification, such as National Institute of Automotive Service Excellence certification, or postsecondary training in automotive selling, such as NADA's CAM program. Dealerships will hire those with proven sales skill in a different field for sales-worker positions and give them on-the-job training.

Employers frequently post job openings at schools that provide postsecondary education in business administration or automotive marketing. Certified automotive technicians or body repairers who think they might eventually like to break into a sales job should look for employment at dealership service centers. They will have frequent contact with sales workers and make connections with dealership managers and owners, as well as become so familiar with one or more models of a manufacturer's cars that they will make well-informed, knowledgeable sales workers.

Some dealerships will hire young workers with little experience in automobile services who can demonstrate proven skills in sales and a willingness to learn. These workers will learn on the job. They may first be given administrative tasks. Eventually, they will accompany experienced sales workers on the showroom floor and learn "hands-on." After about a year, the workers will sell on their own, and managers will evaluate their selling skills in sales meetings and suggest ways they can improve their sales records.

ADVANCEMENT

The longer sales workers stay with a dealership, the larger their client base grows and the more cars are sold. Advancement for many sales workers comes in the form of increased earnings and customer loyalty. Other sales workers may be promoted through a combination of experience and further training or certification.

As positions open, sales workers with proven management skills go on to be assistant and general managers. Managers with excellent sales skills and a good client base may open a new franchise dealership or their own independent dealership.

The Society of Automotive Sales Professionals (SASP), a division of NADA, provides sales workers with advancement possibilities. Once sales workers have completed a certification process and have a minimum of six months' sales experience, they are eligible to participate in SASP seminars that stress improving the new car buying process by polishing a sales worker's professional image.

EARNINGS

Earnings for automobile sales workers vary depending on location, size, and method of salary. Previously, most dealerships paid their sales workers either straight commission or salary plus commission. This forced sales workers to become extremely aggressive in their selling strategies—and often too aggressive for many customers. With a new trend toward pressure-free selling, more sales workers are earning a straight salary. Many dealerships still offer incentives such as bonuses and profit sharing to encourage sales. The average hourly wage for automotive sales workers was $18.61 in 2004, according to the U.S. Department of Labor. Those who work on a straight-commission basis can earn considerably more; however, their earnings are minimal during slow periods. Sales workers just getting started in the field may earn lower annual salaries for a few years as they work to establish a client base. They may start in the low $20,000s. According to the NADA, the average earnings for a new-car dealership employee is $44,676. Benefits vary by dealership but often include health insurance and a paid vacation. An increasing number of employers will pay all or most of an employee's certification training.

WORK ENVIRONMENT

Sales workers for new car dealerships work in pleasant indoor showrooms. Most used car dealerships keep the majority of their cars in outdoor lots where sales workers may spend much of their day. Upon final arrangements for a sale, they work in comfortable office spaces at a desk. Suits are the standard attire. During slow periods, when competition among dealers is fierce, sales workers often work under pressure. They must not allow "lost" sales to discourage their work. The typical workweek is between 40 and 50 hours, although if business is good, a sales worker will work more. Since most customers shop for cars on the weekends and in the evenings, work hours are irregular.

OUTLOOK

Automobile dealerships are one of the businesses most severely affected by economic recession. Conversely, when the economy is strong, the automobile sales industry tends to benefit. For the sales worker, growth, in any percentage, is good news, as they are the so-called front-line professionals in the industry who are responsible for representing the dealerships and manufacturers and for getting their cars out on the streets.

The automobile sales worker faces many future challenges. A shift in customer buying preferences and experience is forcing sales workers to reevaluate their selling methods. Information readily available on the Internet helps customers shop for the most competitive financing or leasing package and read reviews on car and truck models that interest them. Transactions are still brokered at the dealer, but once consumers become more familiar with the Internet, many will shop and buy exclusively from home.

Another trend threatening dealers is the automotive superstore (such as CarMax, AutoNation, and so on) where customers have a large inventory to select from at a base price and get information and ask questions about a car not from a sales worker but from a computer. Sales workers are still needed to finalize the sale, but their traditional role at the dealership is lessened.

Nonetheless, the number of cars and trucks on U.S. roads is expected to increase, and opportunities in this lucrative but stressful career should continue to increase about as fast as the average.

FOR MORE INFORMATION

For information on accreditation and testing, contact
National Automobile Dealers Association
8400 Westpark Drive
McLean, VA 22102-5116
Tel: 800-252-6232
Email: nadainfo@nada.org
http://www.nada.org

For information on certification, contact
National Institute for Automotive Service Excellence
101 Blue Seal Drive SE, Suite 101
Leesburg, VA 20175-5646
Tel: 888-ASE-TEST
http://www.asecert.org

Buyers

OVERVIEW

There are two main types of *buyers. Wholesale buyers* purchase merchandise directly from manufacturers and resell it to retail firms, commercial establishments, and other institutions. *Retail buyers* purchase goods from wholesalers (and occasionally from manufacturers) for resale to the general public. In either case, buyers must understand their customers' needs and be able to purchase goods at an appropriate price and in sufficient quantity. Sometimes a buyer is referred to by the type of merchandise purchased—for example, jewelry buyer or toy buyer. There are approximately 156,000 buyers (nonfarm products) currently working in the United States.

HISTORY

The job of the buyer has been influenced by a variety of historical changes, including the growth of large retail stores in the 20th century. In the past, store owners typically performed almost all of the business activities, including the purchase of merchandise. Large stores, in contrast, had immensely more complicated operations, requiring large numbers of specialized workers such as sales clerks, receiving and shipping clerks, advertising managers, personnel officers, and buyers. The introduction of mass production systems at factories required more complicated planning, ordering, and scheduling of purchases. A wider range of available merchandise also called for more astute selection and purchasing techniques.

QUICK FACTS

School Subjects
Business
Economics
Mathematics

Personal Skills
Helping/teaching
Leadership/management

Work Environment
Primarily indoors
One location with some travel

Minimum Education Level
High school diploma

Salary Range
$24,900 to $42,870 to $80,330+

Certification or Licensing
Voluntary

Outlook
More slowly than the average

DOT
162

GOE
08.01.03

NOC
6233

O*NET-SOC
11-3061.00, 13-1021.00, 13-1022.00

THE JOB

Wholesale and retail buyers are part of a complex system of production, distribution, and merchandising. Both are concerned with recognizing and satisfying the huge variety of consumer needs and desires. Most specialize in acquiring one or two lines of merchandise.

Retail buyers work for retail stores. They generally can be divided into two types: The first, working directly under a merchandise manager, not only purchases goods but directly supervises salespeople. When a new product appears on the shelves, for example, buyers may work with salespeople to point out its distinctive features. This type of retail buyer thus takes responsibility for the products' marketing. The second type of retail buyer is concerned only with purchasing and has no supervisory responsibilities. These buyers cooperate with the sales staff to promote maximum sales.

All retail buyers must understand the basic merchandising policies of their stores. Purchases are affected by the size of the buyer's annual budget, the kind of merchandise needed in each buying season, and trends in the market. Success in buying is directly related to the profit or loss shown by particular departments. Buyers often work with *assistant buyers,* who spend much of their time maintaining sales and inventory records.

All buyers must be experts in the merchandise that they purchase. They order goods months ahead of their expected sale, and they must be able to predetermine marketability based upon cost, style, and competitive items. Buyers must also be well acquainted with the best sources of supply for each product they purchase.

Depending upon the location, size, and type of store, a retail buyer may deal directly with traveling salespeople (ordering from samples or catalogs), order by mail or by telephone directly from the manufacturer or wholesaler, or travel to key cities to visit merchandise showrooms and manufacturing establishments. Most use a combination of these approaches.

Buying trips to such cities as New York, Chicago, and San Francisco are an important part of the work for buyers at a larger store. For specialized products such as glassware, china, liquors, and gloves, some buyers make yearly trips to major European production centers. Sometimes manufacturers of similar items organize trade shows to attract a number of buyers. Buying trips are difficult; a buyer may visit six to eight suppliers in a single day. The buyer must make decisions on the spot about the opportunity for profitable sale of merchandise. Customers' tastes, not how much the buyer personally likes the merchandise, are the important elements. Most buyers operate under an annual purchasing budget for the departments they represent.

Mergers between stores and expansion of individual department stores into chains of stores have created central buying positions. *Central buyers* order in unusually large quantities. As a result, they have the power to develop their own set of specifications for a particular item and ask manufacturers to bid on the right to provide it. Goods purchased by central buyers may be marketed under the manufacturer's label (as is normally done) or ordered with the store's label or a chain brand name.

To meet this competition, independent stores often work with *resident buyers,* who purchase merchandise for a large number of stores. By purchasing large quantities of the same product, resident buyers can obtain the same types of discounts enjoyed by large chain stores and then pass along the savings to their customers.

REQUIREMENTS

High School

A high school diploma generally is required for entering the field of buying. Useful high school courses include mathematics, business, English, and economics.

Postsecondary Training

A college degree may not be a requirement for becoming a buyer, but it is becoming increasingly important, especially for advancement. A majority of buyers have attended college, many majoring in business, engineering, or economics. Some colleges and universities also offer majors in purchasing or materials management. Regardless of the major, useful courses in preparation for a career in buying include accounting, economics, commercial law, finance, marketing, and various business classes such as business communications, business organization and management, and computer applications in business.

Retailing experience is helpful to gain a sense of customer tastes and witness the supply-and-demand process. Additional training is available through trade associations such as the Institute for Supply Management, which sponsors conferences, seminars, and workshops.

Certification or Licensing

Certification, although not required, is becoming increasingly important. Various levels of certification are available through the

American Purchasing Society and the Institute for Supply Management. To earn most certifications, you must have work experience, meet education requirements, and pass written and oral exams.

Other Requirements
If you are interested in becoming a buyer, you should be organized and have excellent decision-making skills. Predicting consumer tastes and keeping stores and wholesalers appropriately stocked requires resourcefulness, good judgment, and confidence. You should also have skills in marketing to identify and promote products that will sell. Finally, leadership skills are needed to supervise assistant buyers and deal with manufacturers' representatives and store executives.

EXPLORING

One way to explore the retailing field is through part-time or summer employment in a store. A good time to look for such work is during the Christmas season. Door-to-door selling is another way to gain business retailing experience. Occasionally, experience in a retail store can be found through special high school programs.

EMPLOYERS

Buyers work for a wide variety of businesses, both wholesale and retail, as well as for government agencies. Employers range from small stores, where buying may be only one function of a manager's

Mean Annual Earnings by Industry, 2005

Employer	Mean Annual Earnings
Management of companies and enterprises	$56,580
Electronic markets and agents and brokers	$54,770
Grocery and related product wholesalers	$47,620
Building material and supplies dealers	$43,610
Grocery stores	$37,120

Source: U.S. Department of Labor

job, to multinational corporations, where a buyer may specialize in one type of item and buy in enormous quantity.

There are approximately 156,000 wholesale and retail buyers (except farm products) employed in the United States. Others work in businesses that provide services and in government agencies.

STARTING OUT

Most buyers find their first job by applying to the personnel office of a retail establishment or wholesaler. Because knowledge of retailing is important, buyers may be required to have work experience in a store.

Most buyers begin their careers as retail sales workers. The next step may be *head of stock*. The head of stock maintains stock inventory records and keeps the merchandise in a neat and well-organized fashion both to protect its value and to permit easy access. He or she usually supervises the work of several employees. This person also works in an intermediate position between the salespeople on the floor and the buyer who provides the merchandise. The next step to becoming a buyer may be assistant buyer. For many department stores, promotion to full buyer requires this background.

Large department stores or chains operate executive training programs for college graduates who seek buying and other retail executive positions. A typical program consists of 16 successive weeks of work in a variety of departments. This on-the-job experience is supplemented by formal classroom work that most often is conducted by senior executives and training department personnel. Following this orientation, trainees are placed in junior management positions for an additional period of supervised experience and training.

ADVANCEMENT

Buyers are key employees of the stores or companies that employ them. One way they advance is through increased responsibility, such as more authority to make commitments for merchandise and more complicated buying assignments.

Buyers are sometimes promoted to *merchandise manager,* which requires them to supervise other buyers, help develop the store's merchandising policies, and coordinate buying and selling activities with related departments. Other buyers may become vice presidents in charge of merchandising or even store presidents. Because buyers learn much about retailing in their job, they are in a position to advance to top executive positions. Some buyers use their knowledge of retailing and the contacts they have developed with suppliers to set up their own businesses.

EARNINGS

How much a buyer earns depends on various factors, including the employer's sales volume. Mass merchandisers such as discount or chain department stores pay among the highest salaries.

The U.S. Department of Labor reports the median annual income for nonagricultural wholesale and retail buyers was $42,870 in 2005. The lowest-paid 10 percent of these buyers made less than $24,900 yearly, and the highest-paid 10 percent earned more than $80,330 annually.

Most buyers receive the usual benefits, such as vacation, sick leave, life and health insurance, and pension plans. Retail buyers may receive cash bonuses for their work and may also receive discounts on merchandise they purchase from their employer.

WORK ENVIRONMENT

Buyers work in a dynamic and sometimes stressful atmosphere. They must make important decisions on an hourly basis. The results of their work, both successes and failures, show up quickly on the profit-and-loss statement.

Buyers frequently work long or irregular hours. Evening and weekend hours are common, especially during the holiday season, when the retail field is at its busiest. Extra hours may be required to bring records up to date, for example, or to review stock and to become familiar with the store's overall marketing design for the coming season. Travel may also be a regular part of a buyer's job, possibly requiring several days away from home each month.

Although buyers must sometimes work under pressure, they usually work in pleasant, well-lit environments. They also benefit from having a diverse set of responsibilities.

OUTLOOK

Employment of wholesale and retail buyers is projected to grow more slowly than the average through 2014, according to the U.S. Department of Labor. Reasons for this decrease include the large number of business mergers and acquisitions, which results in the blending of buying departments and the elimination of redundant jobs. In addition, the use of computers, which increases efficiency, and the trend of some large retail companies to centralize their operations will both contribute to fewer new jobs for buyers. Some job openings will result from the need to hire replacement workers for those who leave the field. On the other hand, companies in the service sector are beginning to realize the advantages of having professional buyers.

FOR MORE INFORMATION

For career information and job listings, contact
American Purchasing Society
8 East Galena Boulevard, Suite 203
Aurora, IL 60506-4161
Tel: 630-859-0250
http://www.american-purchasing.com

For lists of colleges with purchasing programs and career information, contact
Institute for Supply Management
PO Box 22160
Tempe, AZ 85285-2160
Tel: 800-888-6276
http://www.ism.ws

For materials on educational programs in the retail industry, contact
National Retail Federation
325 7th Street NW, Suite 1100
Washington, DC 20004-2818
Tel: 202-783-7971
http://www.nrf.com

Cashiers

QUICK FACTS

School Subjects
Business
Mathematics

Personal Skills
Following instructions
Helping/teaching

Work Environment
Primarily indoors
Primarily one location

Minimum Education Level
High school diploma

Salary Range
$12,440 to $16,260 to
$23,300+

Certification or Licensing
None available

Outlook
More slowly than the
average

DOT
211

GOE
07.03.01

NOC
6611

O*NET-SOC
41-2011.00

OVERVIEW

Cashiers are employed in many different businesses, including supermarkets, department stores, restaurants, and movie theaters. In general, they are responsible for handling money received from customers.

One of the principal tasks of a cashier is operating a cash register. The cash register records all the monetary transactions going into or out of the cashier's workstation. These transactions might involve cash, credit card charges, personal checks, refunds, and exchanges. To assist in inventory control, the cash register often tallies the specific products sold. Approximately 3.5 million cashiers are employed in the United States.

HISTORY

In earlier times, when most stores were small and independently owned, merchants were usually able to take care of most aspects of their businesses, including receiving money from customers. The demand for cashiers increased as large department stores, supermarkets, and self-service stores became more common. Cashiers were hired to receive customers' money, make change, provide customer receipts, and wrap merchandise. Cashiers, who dealt with customers one on one, also became the primary representatives of these businesses.

THE JOB

Although cashiers are employed in many different types of businesses and establishments, most handle the following tasks: receiving money from customers, making change, and providing customers with payment receipts. The type of business dictates other duties. In supermarkets, for example, cashiers might be required to bag groceries. Typically, cashiers in drug or department stores also package or bag merchandise for customers. In currency exchanges, they cash checks, receive utility bill payments, and sell various licenses and permits.

At some businesses, cashiers handle tasks not directly related to customers. Some cashiers, for example, prepare bank deposits for the management. In large businesses, where cashiers are often given a lot of responsibility, they may receive and record cash payments made to the firm and handle payment of the firm's bills. Cashiers might even prepare sales tax reports, compute income tax deductions for employees' pay rates, and prepare paychecks and payroll envelopes.

Cashiers usually operate some type of cash register or other business machine. These machines might print out the amount of each purchase, automatically add the total amount, provide a paper receipt for the customer, and open the cash drawer for the cashier. Other, more complex machines, such as those used in hotels, large department stores, and supermarkets, might print an itemized bill of the customer's purchases. In some cases, cashiers use electronic devices called *optical scanners,* which read the prices of goods from bar codes printed on the merchandise. As the cashier passes the product over the scanner, the scanner reads the code on the product and transmits the code to the cashier's terminal. The price of the item is then automatically displayed at the terminal and added to the customer's bill. Cashiers generally have their own drawer of money, known as a *bank,* which fits into the cash register or terminal. They must keep an accurate record of the amount of money in the drawer. Other machines used by cashiers include adding machines and change-dispensing machines.

Job titles vary depending on where the cashier is employed. In supermarkets, cashiers might be known as *check-out clerks* or *grocery checkers;* in theaters they are often referred to as *ticket sellers* or *box office cashiers;* and in cafeterias they are frequently called *cashier-checkers, food checkers,* or *food tabulators.* In large businesses, cashiers might be given special job titles such as *disbursement clerk, credit cashier,* or *cash accounting clerk.*

In addition to handling money, theater box office cashiers might answer telephone inquiries and operate machines that dispense tickets and change. Restaurant cashiers might receive telephone calls for meal reservations and for special parties, keep the reservation book current, type the menu, stock the sales counter with candies and smoking supplies, and seat customers.

Department store or *supermarket cashiers* typically bag or wrap purchases. During slack periods, they might price the merchandise, restock shelves, make out order forms, and perform other duties similar to those of food and beverage order clerks. Those employed as hotel cashiers usually keep accurate records of telephone charges and room-service bills to go on the customer's account. They might also be in charge of overseeing customers' safe-deposit boxes, handling credit card billing, and notifying room clerks of customer checkouts.

Cashier supervisors, money-room supervisors, and *money counters* might act as cashiers for other cashiers—receiving and recording cash and sales slips from them and making sure their cash registers contain enough money to make change for customers.

REQUIREMENTS

Some employers require that cashiers be at least 18 years of age and have graduated from high school. Employers might also prefer applicants with job experience, the ability to type, or knowledge of

Top 10 U.S. Retailers, 2006 (by revenue)

Name	Revenue	# of Stores
1. Wal-Mart	$315.4 million	6,131
2. Home Depot	$81.5 million	2,042
3. Kroger	$60.5 million	3,726
4. Sears Holdings	$53.9 million	3,770
5. Costco	$52.9 million	461
6. Target	$52.6 million	1,397
7. Lowe's	$43.2 million	1,225
8. Walgreeen	$42.2 million	4,953
9. Albertsons	$40.3 million	2,500
10. Safeway	$38.4 million	1,775

Source: *STORES* magazine

elementary accounting. Cashiers typically receive on-the-job training from experienced employees. In addition, some businesses have special training programs, providing information on the store's history, for example, as well as instruction on store procedures, security measures, and the use of equipment.

High School
High school courses useful to cashiers include bookkeeping, typing, computer science, business machine operation, and business arithmetic.

Postsecondary Training
For more complicated cashier jobs, employers might prefer applicants who are graduates of a two-year community college or business schools. Businesses often fill cashier positions by promoting existing employees, such as clerk-typists, baggers, and ushers.

Other Requirements
Most cashiers have constant personal contact with the public. A pleasant disposition and a desire to serve the public are thus important qualities. Cashiers must also be proficient with numbers and have good hand-eye coordination and finger dexterity. Accuracy is especially important.

Because they handle large sums of money, some cashiers must be able to meet the standards of bonding companies. Bonding companies evaluate applicants for risks and frequently fingerprint applicants for registration and background checks. Not all cashiers are required to be bonded, however.

In some areas, cashiers are required to join a union, but fewer than 20 percent of cashiers are union members. Most union cashiers work in grocery stores and supermarkets and belong to the United Food and Commercial Workers International Union.

EXPLORING

You can try to find part-time employment as a cashier. This will enable you to explore your interest and aptitude for this type of work. You can sometimes obtain related job experience by working in the school bookstore or cafeteria or by participating in community activities such as raffles and sales drives that require the handling of money. It can also be useful to talk with persons already employed as cashiers.

EMPLOYERS

Of the approximately 3.5 million cashiers working in the country, about 27 percent work in food and beverage stores. Large numbers are also employed in restaurants, department stores, and other retail stores, and many work in hotels, theaters, and casinos.

STARTING OUT

People generally enter this field by applying directly to the personnel directors of large businesses or to the managers or owners of small businesses. Applicants may learn of job openings through newspaper help-wanted ads, through friends and business associates, or through school placement agencies. Private or state employment agencies can also help. Employers sometimes require that applicants provide personal references from schools or former employers attesting to their character and personal qualifications.

ADVANCEMENT

Opportunities for advancement vary depending on the size and type of business, personal initiative, experience, and special training and skills. Cashier positions, for example, can provide people with the business skills to move into other types of clerical jobs or managerial positions. Opportunities for promotion are greater within larger firms than in small businesses or stores. Cashiers sometimes advance to cashier supervisors, shift leaders, division managers, or store managers. In hotels, they might be able to advance to room clerks or related positions.

For most people, cashiering is a temporary job. The U.S. Department of Labor noted in 2004 that nearly half of all cashiers were 24 years of age or under.

EARNINGS

New cashiers with no experience are generally paid the minimum wage. Employers can pay workers younger than 20 a lower training wage for up to six months.

Cashiers had median hourly earnings of $7.82 in 2005, according to the U.S. Department of Labor. A cashier working full time at this rate of pay would have a yearly income of approximately $16,260. The department also reports that the lowest-paid 10 percent earned less than $5.98 per hour (about $12,440 annually), and the highest-

A cashier receives payment from a customer. *(Jim Whitmer Photography)*

paid 10 percent made more than $11.20 hourly (about $23,300 per year). Wages are generally higher for union workers; union workers in service occupations were paid about six percent more than non-union. Cashiers employed in restaurants generally earn less than those in other businesses do.

Some cashiers, especially those working for large companies, receive health and life insurance as well as paid vacations and sick days. Some are also offered employee retirement plans or stock option plans. Cashiers are sometimes given merchandise discounts. Benefits are usually available only to full-time employees. Many employers try to save money by hiring part-time cashiers and not paying them benefits.

WORK ENVIRONMENT

Cashiers sometimes work evenings, weekends, and holidays, when many people shop and go out for entertainment. The work of the cashier is usually not too strenuous, but employees often need to stand during most of their working hours. Cashiers must be able to work rapidly and under pressure during rush hours. Handling many items very quickly and dealing with irate customers can be very stressful. Many cashiers complain about repetitive-stress injuries.

Most cashiers work indoors and in rooms that are well ventilated and well lighted. The work area itself, however, can be rather small and confining; cashiers typically work behind counters, in cages or booths, or in other small spaces. Workspaces for cashiers are frequently located near entrances and exits, so cashiers may be exposed to drafts.

OUTLOOK

Employment for cashiers is expected to grow more slowly than the average for all occupations through 2014, according to the U.S. Department of Labor. Despite this prediction, opportunities for cashiers should continue to be good. Not only are we experiencing a changeover to a more and more service-based economy, but the growth of huge retail shopping chains has helped fuel a constant need for cashiers, who are, unfortunately, considered low-paid and disposable workers. Moreover, as a result of a high turnover rate among cashiers, many jobs will become available as workers leaving the field are replaced. Each year, almost one-third of all cashiers leave their jobs for various reasons.

Factors that could limit job growth include the increased use of automatic change-making machines, vending machines, and e-commerce, which could decrease the number of cashiers needed in some business operations. Future job opportunities will be available to those experienced in bookkeeping, typing, business machine operation, and general office skills. Many part-time jobs should also be available. Although nearly half of all cashiers are 24 years of age or younger, many businesses have started diversifying their workforce by hiring older persons and those with disabilities to fill some job openings.

FOR MORE INFORMATION

For information about educational programs in the retail industry, contact
National Retail Federation
325 7th Street, NW, Suite 1100
Washington, DC 20004-2818
Tel: 202-783-7971
http://www.nrf.com

The UFCW represents workers in retail food, meatpacking, poul-
try, and other food processing industries. For more information,
contact

United Food and Commercial Workers International Union
(UFCW)
1775 K Street NW
Washington, DC 20006-1502
Tel: 202-223-3111
http://www.ufcw.org

Computer and Electronics Sales Representatives

OVERVIEW

Computer and electronics sales representatives sell hardware, software, peripheral computer equipment, and electronics equipment to customers in retail stores. Sometimes they follow up sales with installation of systems, maintenance, or training of the customer.

HISTORY

The first major advances in modern computer technology were made during World War II. After the war, people thought that computers were too big (they easily filled entire warehouses) to ever be used for anything other than government projects, such as their use in compiling the 1950 census.

The introduction of semiconductors to computer technology made smaller and less expensive computers possible. The semiconductors replaced the bigger, slower vacuum tubes of the first computers. These changes made it easier for businesses to adapt computers to their needs, which they began doing as early as 1954. Within 30 years, computers had revolutionized the way people worked, played, and even shopped. Few occupations have remained untouched by this technological revolution. Consequently, computers are found in businesses, government offices, hospitals, schools, science labs, and homes. Clearly, there is a huge market for the sale of computers and peripheral equipment. There is an important need today for knowledgeable sales representatives to educate the retail public about these products.

THE JOB

The first step in the selling process is customer consultation. Sales representatives determine the customer's current technological needs as well as those of the future. Most stores have the latest computer and electronics products on display so that customers can test the products themselves. During consultation, reps demonstrate the technology's value and how well it will perform. Often, customers do not have expertise in computer or electronics technology, so the rep must explain and translate complicated computer tech-talk as well as answer numerous questions. When a customer decides to make a purchase, the sales representative makes out a sales check; receives payment; gives change and a receipt; and bags the purchase or, if it is a large product, arranges for delivery to the individual's vehicle or home.

Some retail stores may offer installation services to their customers. In this instance, sales representatives travel to a customer's home to install the hardware or software and ensure that it is operating properly.

In addition to waiting on customers, sales representatives are responsible for restocking inventory, preparing window displays and other signage, and rearranging merchandise for sale. They may also attend regular staff meetings to improve their sales skills and learn about the latest products.

REQUIREMENTS

High School
Classes in speech and writing will help you learn how to communicate your product to large groups of people. Computer science and electronics classes will give you a basic overview of the field. General business and math classes will also be helpful.

Postsecondary Training
Prepare yourself for a career in this field by developing your computer knowledge. Take computer and math classes, as well as business classes to help develop a sound business sense. Since sales representatives must explain sometimes complicated technologies to customers, excellent communications skills are a must. Hone yours by taking English and speech classes.

In this particular field of sales, extensive computer knowledge is just as important as business savvy. Most computer sales representatives pursue computer science courses concurrently with their business classes. Such training can be obtained through special work training seminars, adult education classes, or courses at a technical school. Many companies require their sales staff to complete a training program where they'll learn the technologies and work tools needed for the job. (This is where you'll pick up the techno-speak for your specific field.)

Other Requirements

As important as having computer and electronics knowledge is having a "sales" personality. Sales representatives must be confident and knowledgeable about themselves as well as the product they are selling. They should have strong interpersonal skills and enjoy dealing with all types of people, from families buying their first PC, to individuals with extensive computer knowledge. They should also be neat and well groomed and have a pleasant personality.

EXPLORING

To learn more about the day-to-day activities of a computer and electronic sales representative, visit computer stores and watch how the workers serve the customers. Ask a sales representative if he or she is willing to answer a few of your questions about what they do. Keep an eye on newspaper advertisements and circulars to find out what the latest hot items are on sale. Make a point of getting to know as much as possible about the items currently on the market and make a note of their key features. Visit manufacturers to find out how the companies are presenting their products to the public.

EMPLOYERS

Sales representatives work in many types of retail establishments that sell computers and other electronic devices such as stereos, digital cameras, computer and video game platforms, camcorders, DVD players, MP3 players, cell phones, and PDAs. Major employers include Best Buy, Office Depot, Staples, Circuit City, Fry's Electronics, CompUSA, and Wal-Mart.

STARTING OUT

Contact local computer and electronic stores near you to see if they have available positions. Other avenues to try when conducting your job search include newspaper job ads and the Internet. Many retailers maintain Web sites where they post employment opportunities as well as receive online resumes and applications. Your school's career services office is a great place to start your job search. Not only will the counselors have information on jobs not advertised in the paper, but they can provide tips on resume writing and interviewing techniques.

ADVANCEMENT

With a good work record, a computer or electronics sales representative may be offered a position in management. A manager is responsible for supervising the sales for a given retail store or an entire region. A management position comes with not only a higher salary but a higher level of responsibility as well. An effective manager should be well versed in the company's product and selling techniques. Those already at the management level may decide to transfer to the marketing side of the business. Positions in marketing may involve planning the marketing strategy for a new computer or electronics product or line and coordinating sales campaigns and product distribution.

EARNINGS

Sales representatives working in retail are paid an hourly wage, usually minimum wage ($5.15 an hour), which may be supplemented with commissions based on a percentage of sales made that day or week. Salaries are also dependent on the product sold (PCs, mainframes, peripherals) and the market served.

According to the U.S. Department of Labor, median earnings for all retail sales workers, including commissions, was $25,890 in 2005. At the bottom of the pay scale were those making less than $13,590 annually, and at the top were those who made more than $37,250 annually. Most computer sales representatives working for large employers are offered a benefits package including health and life insurance, paid holidays and vacations, and continuing education and training, as well as volume bonuses or stock options.

WORK ENVIRONMENT

Retail sales representatives typically work 40 hours a week, though longer hours may be necessary during busy shopping seasons. Whether or not the sales representative is compensated during these extended hours varies from store to store. However, increased work

A computer sales representative explains the features of a laptop computer to a young couple. *(Tomas del Amo, Index Stock Imagery)*

times usually mean increased sales volume, which in the end translates to more commissions. Retail representatives must be prepared to deal with a large volume of customers with varying levels of technical knowledge, all with many questions. It is necessary to treat customers with respect and patience, regardless of the size of the sale or when there is no sale at all.

OUTLOOK

Employment opportunities for all retail sales representatives are expected to grow about as fast as the average for all occupations through 2014, according to the U.S. Department of Labor.

As computer companies continue to price their products competitively, more and more people will be able to afford new home computer systems or upgrade existing ones with the latest hardware, software, and peripherals. Increased retail sales will increase the need for competent and knowledgeable sales representatives. Many jobs exist at retail giants (Best Buy and Office Depot, known for office-related supplies and equipment, are two examples) that provide consumers with good price packages as well as optional services such as installation and maintenance.

Employment opportunities can also be found with computer specialty stores and consulting companies that deal directly with businesses and their corporate computer and application needs. Computers have become an almost indispensable tool for running a successful business, be it an accounting firm, a public relations company, or a multiphysician medical practice. As long as this trend continues, knowledgeable sales representatives will be needed to bring the latest technological advances in hardware and software to the consumer and corporate level.

All sales workers are adversely affected by economic downturns. In a weak economy, consumers purchase fewer expensive items, and businesses look for ways to trim costs. This results in less of a demand for computers, computer accessories, and electronics and a reduced need for sales workers.

FOR MORE INFORMATION

For information on internships, student membership, and the student magazine, Crossroads, *contact*
Association for Computing Machinery
2 Penn Plaza, Suite 701
New York, NY 10121-0701
Tel: 800-342-6626
Email: SIGS@acm.org
http://www.acm.org

For industry or membership information, contact
North American Retail Dealers Association
4700 West Lake Avenue
Glenview, IL 60025
Tel: 800-621-0298
Email: jevans@narda.com
http://www.narda.com

Counter and Retail Clerks

QUICK FACTS

School Subjects
English
Mathematics
Speech

Personal Skills
Following instructions
Helping/teaching

Work Environment
Primarily indoors
Primarily one location

Minimum Education Level
High school diploma

Salary Range
$13,170 to $18,970 to
$35,950+

Certification or Licensing
None available

Outlook
Faster than the average

DOT
279

GOE
09.05.01

NOC
1453

O*NET-SOC
41-2021.00

OVERVIEW

Counter and retail clerks work as intermediaries between the general public and businesses that provide goods and services. They take orders and receive payments for such services as videotape and DVD rentals, automobile rentals, and laundry and dry cleaning. They often assist customers with their purchasing or rental decisions, especially when sales personnel are not available. These workers might also prepare billing statements, keep records of receipts and sales, and balance money in their cash registers. There are more than 451,000 counter and retail clerks working in the United States.

HISTORY

The first retail outlets in the United States sold food staples, farm necessities, and clothing, and many also served as the post office and became the social and economic centers of their communities. Owners of these general stores often performed all the jobs in the business.

Over the years, retailing has undergone numerous changes. Large retail stores, requiring many workers, including counter and retail clerks, became more common. Also emerging were specialized retail or chain outlets—clothing stores, bicycle shops, computer shops, video stores, and athletic footwear boutiques—which also needed counter and retail clerks to assist customers and to receive payment for services or products.

THE JOB

Job duties vary depending on the type of business. In a shoe repair shop, for example, the clerk receives the shoes to be repaired or cleaned from the customer, examines the shoes, gives a price quote and a receipt to the customer, and then sends the shoes to the work department for the necessary repairs or cleaning. The shoes are marked with a tag specifying what work needs to be done and to whom the shoes belong. After the work is completed, the clerk returns the shoes to the customer and collects payment.

In stores where customers rent equipment or merchandise, clerks prepare rental forms and quote rates to customers. Clerks answer customer questions about the operation of equipment. They often take a deposit to cover any accidents or possible damage. Clerks also check equipment to be certain it is in good working order and make minor adjustments, if necessary. With long-term rentals, such as storage-facility rentals, clerks notify the customers when the rental period is about to expire and when the rent is overdue. *Video-rental clerks* greet customers, check out tapes, and accept payment. Upon return of the tapes, clerks check the condition of the tapes and then put them back on the shelves.

In smaller shops with no sales personnel or in situations when the sales personnel are unavailable, counter and retail clerks assist customers with purchases or rentals by demonstrating the merchandise, answering customers' questions, accepting payment, recording sales, and wrapping the purchases or arranging for their delivery.

In addition to these duties, clerks sometimes prepare billing statements to be sent to customers. They might keep records of receipts and sales throughout the day and balance the money in their registers when their work shift ends. They sometimes are responsible for the display and presentation of products in their store. In supermarkets and grocery stores, clerks stock shelves and bag food purchases for customers.

Service-establishment attendants work in various types of businesses, such as a laundry, where attendants take clothes to be cleaned or repaired and write down the customer's name and address. *Watch-and-clock-repair clerks* receive clocks and watches for repair and examine the timepieces to estimate repair costs. They might make minor repairs, such as replacing a watchband; otherwise, the timepiece is forwarded to the repair shop with a description of needed repairs.

Many clerks have job titles that describe what they do and where they work. These include laundry-pricing clerks; photo-finishing-

A retail clerk at a hardware store checks the availability of a part for a customer. *(Stewart Cohen, Index Stock Imagery)*

counter clerks; tool-and-equipment-rental clerks; airplane-charter clerks; baby-stroller and wheelchair-rental clerks; storage-facility-rental clerks; boat-rental clerks; hospital-television-rental clerks; trailer-rental clerks; automobile-rental clerks; fur-storage clerks; and self-service-laundry and dry-cleaning attendants.

REQUIREMENTS

High School
High school courses useful for the job include English, speech, and mathematics, as well as any business-related classes such as typing, computer science, and those covering principles in retailing. Although there are no specific educational requirements for clerk positions, most employers prefer to hire high school graduates. Legible handwriting and the ability to add and subtract numbers quickly are also necessary.

Other Requirements
To be a counter and retail clerk, you should have a pleasant personality and an ability to interact with a variety of people. You should also be neat and well groomed and have a high degree of personal

responsibility. Counter and retail clerks must be able to adjust to alternating periods of heavy and light activity. No two days—or even customers—are alike. Because some customers can be rude or even hostile, you must exercise tact and patience at all times.

EXPLORING

There are numerous opportunities for part-time or temporary work as a clerk, especially during the holiday season. Many high schools have developed work-study programs that combine courses in retailing with part-time work in the field. Store owners cooperating in these programs may hire you as a full-time worker after you complete the course.

EMPLOYERS

Of the numerous types of clerks working in the United States, approximately 451,000 work as counter and rental clerks at video rental stores, dry cleaners, car rental agencies, and other such establishments. These are not the only employers of clerks, however; hardware stores, shoe stores, moving businesses, camera stores—in fact, nearly any business that sells goods or provides services to the general public employs clerks. Many work on a part-time basis.

STARTING OUT

If you are interested in securing an entry-level position as a clerk, you should contact stores directly. Workers with some experience, such as those who have completed a work-study program in high school, should have the greatest success, but most entry-level positions do not require experience. Jobs are often listed in help-wanted advertisements.

Most stores provide new workers with on-the-job training in which experienced clerks explain company policies and procedures and teach new employees how to operate the cash register and other necessary equipment. This training usually continues for several weeks until the new employee feels comfortable on the job.

ADVANCEMENT

Counter and retail clerks usually begin their employment doing routine tasks such as checking stock and operating the cash register. With experience, they might advance to more complicated assignments and assume some sales responsibilities. Those with the skill and aptitude might become salespeople or store managers, although further education is normally required for management positions.

The high turnover rate in the clerk position increases the opportunities for being promoted. The number and kind of opportunities, however, depend on the place of employment and the ability, training, and experience of the employee.

EARNINGS

According to the U.S. Department of Labor, the median hourly wage for counter and rental clerks was $9.12 in 2005. Working year round at 40 hours per week, a clerk earning this wage would make approximately $18,970 annually. Ten percent of counter and rental clerks earned less than $6.33 per hour (approximately $13,170 annually) in 2005, and 10 percent earned more than $17.28 per hour (or $35,950 annually). Wages among clerks vary for a number of reasons, including the industry in which they work. The Department of Labor reports, for example, that those working in the automobile rental field had mean hourly earnings of $11.52 (approximately $23,960 per year) in 2005, while those in dry cleaning and laundry services earned a median of $8.13 per hour (approximately $16,910 yearly). Wages also vary among clerks due to factors such as size of the business, location in the country, and experience of the employee.

Those workers who have union affiliation (usually those who work for supermarkets) may earn considerably more than their non-union counterparts. Full-time workers, especially union members, might also receive benefits such as paid vacation time and health insurance, but this is not the industry norm. Some businesses offer merchandise discounts for their employees. Part-time workers usually receive fewer benefits than those working full time.

WORK ENVIRONMENT

Although a 40-hour workweek is common, many stores operate on a 44- to 48-hour workweek. Most stores are open on Saturday and many on Sunday. Most stores are also open one or more weekday evenings, so a clerk's working hours might vary from week to week and include evening and weekend shifts. Many counter and retail clerks work overtime during Christmas and other rush seasons. Part-time clerks generally work during peak business periods.

Most clerks work indoors in well-ventilated and well-lighted environments. The job can be routine and repetitive, and clerks often spend much of their time on their feet.

OUTLOOK

The U.S. Department of Labor predicts that employment for counter and rental clerks will grow faster than the average for all occupations through 2014. Businesses that focus on customer service will always want to hire friendly and responsible clerks. Major employers should be those providing rental products and services, such as car rental firms, video rental stores, and other equipment rental businesses. Because of the high turnover in this field, however, many job openings will come from the need to replace workers. Opportunities for temporary or part-time work should be good, especially during busy business periods. Employment opportunities for clerks are plentiful in large metropolitan areas, where their services are in great demand.

FOR MORE INFORMATION

For information on scholarships and internships, contact
Retail Industry Leaders Association
1700 North Moore Street, Suite 2250
Arlington, VA 22209-1933
Tel: 703-841-2300
http://www.retail-leaders.org/new/index.aspx

For information about careers in the retail industry, contact
National Retail Federation
325 7th Street NW, Suite 1100
Washington, DC 20004-2818
Tel: 800-673-4692
http://www.nrf.com

Customer Service Representatives

OVERVIEW

Customer service representatives, sometimes called *customer care representatives,* work with customers of one or many companies, assist with customer problems, or answer questions. Customer service representatives work in many different industries to provide "front-line" customer service in a variety of businesses. Most customer service representatives work in an office setting, though some may work in the "field" to better meet customer needs. There are approximately 2.1 million customer service representatives employed in the United States.

HISTORY

Customer service has been a part of business for many years; however, the formal title of customer service representative is relatively new. More than a decade ago, the International Customer Service Association established Customer Service Week to recognize and promote customer service.

As the world moves toward a more global and competitive economic market, customer service, along with quality control, has taken a front seat in the business world. Serving customers and serving them well is more important now than ever before.

Customer service is about communication, so progress in customer service can be tied closely to progress in the communication industry. When Alexander Graham Bell invented the telephone in 1876, he probably did not envision the customer service lines, automated response messages, and toll-free phone numbers that now help customer service representatives do their jobs.

The increased use of the Internet has helped companies serve and communicate with their customers in another way. From the simple email complaint form to online help files, companies are using the Internet to provide better customer service. Some companies even have online chat capabilities to communicate with their customers instantaneously on the Web.

THE JOB

Julie Cox is a customer service representative for Affina, a call center that handles customer service for a variety of companies. Cox works with each of Affina's clients and the call center operators to ensure that each call-in receives top customer service.

Customer service representatives often handle complaints and problems, and Cox finds that to be the case at the call center as well. While the operators who report to her provide customer service to those on the phone, Cox must oversee that customer service while also keeping in mind the customer service for her client, whatever business they may be in.

"I make sure that the clients get regular reports of the customer service calls and check to see if there are any recurring problems," says Cox.

One of the ways Cox observes whether customer service is not being handled effectively is by monitoring the actual time spent on each phone call. If an operator spends a lot of time on a call, there is most likely a problem.

"Our customers are billed per minute," says Cox. "So we want to make sure their customer service is being handled well and efficiently."

Affina's call center in Columbus, Indiana, handles dozens of toll-free lines. While some calls are likely to be focused on complaints or questions, some are easier to handle. Cox and her staff handle calls from people simply wanting to order literature or brochures or to find their nearest dealer location.

Customer service representatives work in a variety of fields and business, but one thing is common—the customer. All businesses depend on their customers to keep them in business, so customer service, whether handled internally or outsourced to a call center like Affina, is extremely important.

Some customer service representatives, like Cox, do most of their work on the telephone. Others may represent companies in the field, where the customer is actually using the product or service. Still other customer service representatives may specialize in Internet service, assisting customers over the Web via email or online chats.

Affina's call center is available to clients 24 hours a day, seven days a week, so Cox and her staff must keep around-the-clock shifts. Not all customer service representatives work a varied schedule; many work a traditional daytime shift. However, customers have problems, complaints, and questions 24 hours a day, so many companies do staff their customer service positions for a longer number of hours, especially to accommodate customers during evenings and weekends.

REQUIREMENTS

High School

A high school diploma is required for most customer service representative positions. High school courses that emphasize communication, such as English and speech, will help you learn to communicate clearly. Any courses that require collaboration with others will also help to teach diplomacy and tact—two important aspects of customer service. Business courses will help you get a good overview of the business world, which is dependent on customers and customer service. Computer skills are also very important.

Postsecondary Training

While a college degree is not necessary to become a customer service representative, certain areas of postsecondary training are helpful. Courses in business and organizational leadership will help to give you a better feel for the business world. Just as in high school, communications classes are helpful in learning to effectively talk with and meet the needs of other people.

These courses can be taken during a college curriculum or may be offered at a variety of customer service workshops or classes. Julie Cox is working as a customer service representative while she earns her business degree from a local college. Along with her college work, she has taken advantage of seminars and workshops to improve her customer service skills.

Bachelor's degrees in business and communications are increasingly required for managerial positions.

Certification or Licensing

Although it is not a requirement, customer service representatives can become certified. The International Customer Service Association offers a manager-level certification program. Upon completion of the program, managers receive the certified customer service professional designation.

Other Requirements

"The best and the worst parts of being a customer service representative are the people," Julie Cox says. Customer service representatives should have the ability to maintain a pleasant attitude at all times, even while serving angry or demanding customers.

A successful customer service representative will most likely have an outgoing personality and enjoy working with people and assisting them with their questions and problems.

Because many customer service representatives work in offices and on the telephone, people with physical disabilities may find this career to be both accessible and enjoyable.

EXPLORING

Julie Cox first discovered her love for customer service while working in retail at a local department store. Explore your ability for customer service by getting a job that deals with the public on a day-to-day basis. Talk with people who work with customers and customer service every day; find out what they like and dislike about their jobs.

There are other ways that you can prepare for a career in this field while you are still in school. Join your school's business club to get a feel for what goes on in the business world today. Doing volunteer work for a local charity or homeless shelter can help you decide if serving others is something you'd enjoy doing as a career.

Evaluate the customer service at the businesses you visit. What makes that salesperson at The Gap better than the operator you talked with last week? Volunteer to answer phones at an agency in your town or city. Most receptionists in small companies and agencies are called on to provide customer service to callers. Try a nonprofit organization; they will welcome the help, and you will get a firsthand look at customer service.

EMPLOYERS

Customer service representatives are hired at all types of companies in a variety of areas. Because all businesses rely on customers, customer service is generally a high priority for those businesses. Some companies, like call centers, may employ a large number of customer service representatives to serve a multitude of clients, while small businesses may simply have one or two people responsible for customer service.

Approximately 30 percent of customer service representatives are employed in four states (California, Texas, Florida, and New York), but opportunities are available throughout the United States. In the United States, approximately 2.1 million workers are employed as customer service representatives.

STARTING OUT

You can become a customer service representative as an entry-level applicant, although some customer service representatives have first served in other areas of a company. Company experience may provide them with more knowledge and experience to answer customer questions. A college degree is not required, but any postsecondary training will increase your ability to find a job in customer service.

Ads for customer service job openings are readily available in newspapers and on Internet job search sites. With some experience and a positive attitude, it is possible to move into the position of customer service representative from another job within the company. Julie Cox started out at Affina as an operator and quickly moved into a customer service capacity.

ADVANCEMENT

Customer service experience is valuable in any business career path. Julie Cox hopes to combine her customer service experience with a business degree and move to the human resources area of her company.

It is also possible to advance to management or marketing jobs after working as a customer service representative. Businesses and their customers are inseparable, so most business professionals are experts at customer relations.

EARNINGS

Earnings vary based on location, level of experience, and size and type of employer. The U.S. Department of Labor reports the median annual income for all customer service representatives as $27,490 in 2005. Salaries ranged from less than $17,820 to more than $44,790.

The Association of Support Professionals, which conducts salary surveys of tech support workers at PC software companies, reports that customer service representatives earned a median annual wage of $35,000 in 2005.

Other benefits vary widely according to the size and type of company in which representatives are employed. Benefits may include medical, dental, vision, and life insurance; 401(k) plans; or bonus incentives. Full-time customer service representatives can expect to receive vacation and sick pay, while part-time workers may not be offered these benefits.

WORK ENVIRONMENT

Customer service representatives work primarily indoors, although some may work in the field where the customers are using the product or service. They usually work in a supervised setting and report to a manager. They may spend many hours on the telephone, answering mail, or handling Internet communication. Many of the work hours involve little physical activity.

While most customer service representatives generally work a 40-hour workweek, others work a variety of shifts. Many businesses want customer service hours to coincide with the times that their customers are available to call or contact the business. For many companies, these times are in the evenings and on the weekends, so some customer service representatives work a varied shift and odd hours.

OUTLOOK

The U.S. Department of Labor predicts that employment for customer service representatives will grow faster than the average for all occupations through 2014. This is a large field of workers and many replacement workers are needed each year as customer service reps leave this job for other positions, retire, or leave for other reasons. In addition, the Internet and e-commerce should increase the need for customer service representatives who will be needed to help customers navigate Web sites, answer questions over the phone, and respond to emails.

For customer service representatives with specific knowledge of a product or business, the outlook is very good, as quick, efficient customer service is valuable in any business. Additional training and education will also make finding a job as a customer service representative an easier task.

FOR MORE INFORMATION

For information on customer service and other support positions, contact

Association of Support Professionals
122 Barnard Avenue
Watertown, MA 02472-3414
Tel: 617-924-3944
http://www.asponline.com

For information on jobs, training, workshops, and salaries, contact

Customer Care Institute
17 Dean Overlook NW
Atlanta, GA 30318-1663
Tel: 404-352-9291
Email: info@customercare.com
http://www.customercare.com

For information about the customer service industry, contact

HDI
102 South Tejon, Suite 1200
Colorado Springs, CO 80903-2242
Tel: 800-248-5667
Email: support@thinkhdi.com
http://www.helpdeskinst.com

For information on international customer service careers, contact

International Customer Service Association
401 North Michigan Avenue
Chicago, IL 60611-4255
Tel: 800-360-4272
Email: icsa@smithbucklin.com
http://www.icsa.com

Florists

OVERVIEW

Florists, or *floral designers,* arrange live or cut flowers, potted plants, foliage, or other decorative items, according to basic design principles to make eye-pleasing creations. Designers make such arrangements for birthdays, weddings, funerals, or other occasions. They are employed by local flower shops or larger national chains, grocery stores, or established at-home businesses. There are over 98,000 floral design workers employed in the United States.

HISTORY

Flowers have been used for centuries as decoration, personal adornment, or for religious purposes. Ancient Egyptians used flowers to honor their many gods and goddesses. Flowers were arranged in low bowls in an orderly, repetitive pattern—flower, bud, foliage, and so on. Special spouted vases were also used to hold flowers. Lotus flowers, also called water lilies, were Egyptian favorites. They came to symbolize sacredness and were associated with Isis, the Egyptian nature goddess. Flowers were sometimes used as decorations for the body, collar, and hair.

Flowers were fashioned into elaborate wreaths and garlands by the ancient Greeks. The best wreathmakers were often commissioned by wealthy Greeks to make wreaths for gifts, awards, or decoration. Chaplets, special wreaths for the head, were especially popular. Cornucopias, horn-shaped containers still used today, were filled with arrangements of flowers, fruits, and vegetables. Flowers arranged into wreaths and garlands were also popular during the Roman period and well through to the Middle Ages.

The Victorian era saw great developments in the art of floral design. There was enormous enthusiasm for flowers, plants, and gardens; the most cultured young ladies were often schooled in the art of flower arrangement. Rules were first established regarding function and design. Magazines and books about floral arrangement were also published during this time. Proper Victorian ladies often had fresh nosegays, or tussie-mussies, a handheld arrangement of tightly knotted flowers, for sentimental reasons, if not to freshen the air. Posy holders, fancy carriers for these small floral arrangements, soon came into fashion. Some were made of ivory, glass, or mother-of-pearl and were elaborately decorated with jewels or etchings. Flowers were also made into small arrangements and tucked into a lady's décolletage inside aptly named containers: bosom bottles.

Ikebana, the Japanese art of floral arrangement created in the sixth century, has been a principal influence on formal flower arrangement design. Its popularity continues today. In the 1950s, free-form expression developed, incorporating pieces of driftwood and figurines within arrangements of flowers and live plants.

Floral traditions of the past still have an impact on us today. It is still fashionable to mark special occasions with flowers, be it an anniversary, wedding, or birthday. People continue to use flowers to commemorate the dead. Today's floral arrangements reflect current styles, trends, and tastes. The best floral designers will follow the developing fashions and creatively adapt them to their arrangements.

THE JOB

From simple birthday bouquets to lavish wedding arrangements, floral designers define a sentiment or mood or make an impression by using flowers as their medium of expression. Along with live flowers, designers may use silk flowers or foliage, fresh fruit, and twigs or incorporate decorative items such as candles, balloons, ribbons, and stuffed animals to their arrangements. Good equipment—foam, wire, wooden or plastic picks, shears, florist's knife, tape, and a variety of containers—is essential. Techniques such as wiring flower stems or shading the tips of blooms with paint or glitter are often used to give floral arrangements a finished look. Familiarity with different species of flowers and plants and creativity and knowledge of the elements of design distinguish a good floral designer.

Floral designers are fortunate to have a number of employment paths from which to choose. Some designers are employed at flower shops, while some opt to work independently. Aurora Gagni, owner of Floral Elegance, is one such entrepreneur. A registered nurse by training but creative by nature, Gagni always enjoyed making crafts. "I would see a picture of a flower arrangement in a magazine and try to duplicate it," she says, "but I would always add and experiment and make it my own creation." Gagni made floral arrangements, wreaths, and displays for family, friends, and coworkers, who in turn would spread word of her abilities. "At one point, I found myself giving bow-making lessons at work!" In time, Gagni had a steady and growing number of customers who relied on her skills.

What persuaded Gagni to give up nursing and go into business for herself? "My kids!" she answers. Indeed, this job perk is an attractive one, especially for someone juggling a career with family: Gagni conducts her business almost entirely from her home and is available for the "many little things"—driving to and from sports events, delivering forgotten lunch boxes, and, of course, homework.

Gagni tackles a variety of floral requests, but weddings are her specialty. While a typical wedding day lasts a few hours, the planning stage can take months. "Usually, the bride and groom look at my book," Gagni says, "and decide if they like my work." If so, the contract is "closed"—the contract agreement is signed, a budget is set, and a down payment is made—several months before the wedding day. Soon after, designs are made, keeping the budget in mind. Many brides wish for orchids with a carnation budget. "I try to accommodate what type of flower or color or look the customer wants," Gagni explains, sometimes making alternate suggestions, especially if price is an issue or if the flower is difficult to obtain. Gagni orders necessary supplies weeks in advance and scouts for upcoming sales. She notifies her floral wholesalers in advance of any flowers that are seasonal or difficult to obtain. Also, she visits the church and reception hall to check on details such as size, location, and any restrictions. The quickest route to both destinations is also mapped out to ensure prompt delivery of the flowers.

Gagni periodically checks in with the bride about any last-minute changes. Oftentimes, more corsages or more banquet table centerpieces are needed to accommodate extra guests. Bows are tied and secured with wire about two weeks before the wedding. Three days before the wedding, flowers are picked and kept fresh in buckets of water treated with floral preservatives. The actual arranging, done in Gagni's basement, is begun the night before the wedding—bricks

A florist prepares an arrangement for a birthday party. *(PhotoDisc)*

of floral foam, treated with water and preservatives, keep the flowers in place. Bouquets and corsages are delivered to the bride's home on the morning of the wedding; and ribbons, flower arrangements, and corsages for the groom's party are brought to the location of the ceremony. Gagni then goes to the hall to set up for the reception. Final touch-ups are given to table centerpieces, the head table is decorated, and the last details are tackled.

Gagni hires additional help for large contracts, especially to assist with the final arrangements. Her children also help when needed, and her husband is her unofficial delivery driver.

Most retail floral businesses keep a relatively small staff. Sales workers help customers place their orders; they also take care of phone orders. Drivers are hired to make deliveries. Sometimes assistant designers are employed.

REQUIREMENTS

High School

Take art and design classes while in high school. After all, "creativity" is an important buzzword in this industry. Biology classes would be helpful in learning about plants and flowers. Do you have aspirations of owning a flower establishment? Sign up for business-related courses and computer classes—they will help make you a better entrepreneur.

Postsecondary Training

In the past, floral designers learned their craft on the job, usually working as an assistant or apprentice to an experienced designer. Most designers today, however, pursue advanced education resulting in a certificate or degree. While this education is not mandatory in the industry, it does give candidates an advantage when they apply for design positions. There are numerous universities that offer degrees in floriculture and horticulture, as well as community colleges and independent schools that offer certification in floral design.

Programs vary from school to school, lasting anywhere from days to years, depending on the type of degree or certificate. The American Floral Art School, a state-approved and licensed vocational school in Chicago, offers courses in modern floral design, with class schedules from one to three weeks. The curriculum includes the fundamentals of artistic floral design; general instruction in picking or wiring, tinting, and arranging flowers; different types of arrangements and their containers; fashion flowers and wedding flowers; and flower shop management. When you are choosing a school to attend, consider the course offerings as well as your career goals. For example, the Boston-based Rittners School of Floral Design offers classes that emphasize floral business skills, a must if you plan on starting your own shop. Some distance education is also available. The Society of American Florists, headquartered in Virginia, has an online learning center through which various courses are offered. (See the end of this article for contact information.)

Other Requirements

Most people don't wake up one morning and decide to become a floral designer. If you don't have creative and artistic inclinations, you're already a step behind the rest. A good floral designer enjoys and understands plants and flowers and can visualize a creation from the very first daffodil. Are you able to work well under pressure and deadlines and effectively deal with vendors or wholesalers? These are daily requirements of the job. Also, be prepared to greet and accommodate all types of customers, from impatient grooms to nervous brides to grieving families. A compassionate and patient personality will help you go far in this field.

EXPLORING

Considering a future in floral design? Now is the best time to determine if this career is the right one for you. As a high school student without experience, it's doubtful you'll be hired as a floral designer; but working as a cashier, flower delivery person, or assistant is a great way to break into the industry.

What about taking some classes to test your talent? Michaels, a national arts and crafts retailer, offers floral design workshops. Look for similar workshops in your area. Park district programs also have design classes, especially during the holiday seasons. Such programs are relatively inexpensive—most times the fee is just enough to cover materials used in class.

Learn the industry firsthand—why not spend a day at work with a floral designer? Explain your interest to your local florist and ask if he or she would be willing to let you observe.

EMPLOYERS

Approximately 98,000 floral designers are employed in the United States. Small, independently owned flower shops are the most common employers of florists. National chains such as Teleflora and FTD supply additional jobs. Flower departments, now a staple in larger grocery stores, also employ floral designers. Approximately 33 percent of floral designers are self-employed.

STARTING OUT

Some floral designers get their start by working as assistant designers. Others, especially if they are certified, may be hired as floral designers. Experienced designers may concentrate in a certain area such as weddings and become wedding specialists.

Aurora Gagni needed to apply for a tax identification number before she officially "opened" her business. This number is necessary to establish accounts with wholesalers and greenhouses, as well as for tax purposes. It would be wise to consult with business or legal experts regarding income tax issues, promotion and advertising, and other matters dealing with operating your own business.

Professionals in floral design maintain a portfolio of their best designs. A portfolio is useful when applying for membership in floral associations, classes, and when wooing potential clients.

ADVANCEMENT

Advancement in this field depends on the interest of the individual. Some floral designers are content to work at small local shops, especially if they have created a name for themselves in the area they serve. Others decide to try employment with larger national chains such as Teleflora or 1-800-FLOWERS. Superstore grocery chains now boast full-service floral departments, creating many job opportunities for designers.

Do you possess an entrepreneurial nature? Maybe owning a floral business—either based in your home or established in the middle of your town's business district—is in your future. Still other options include entering the field of landscape design; interior landscaping for offices, shopping centers, and hotels; or a large floral design specialty. Imagine working on a float for Pasadena's Tournament of Roses Parade.

Many of Aurora Gagni's contracts are for weddings, so it makes sense that her business branches out accordingly. Party favors, cake toppers, and the veil and cord—elements unique in many ethnic wedding ceremonies—are some items Gagni customizes for her clients.

EARNINGS

Experience counts for a lot when it comes to a designer's salary. Geographic location also plays a part in salary differences. Floral designers on the East and West Coasts traditionally enjoy higher-than-average salaries compared to floral designers in other parts of the United States. Stores located in large urban areas tend to have higher annual sales than those in rural areas, resulting in higher pay for their employees.

According to the U.S. Department of Labor, florists had median annual earnings of $21,060 in 2005. Well-established floral designers with a steady customer base can earn more than $32,960 annually. Less experienced florists may earn less than $14,710 annually. The department also reports that florists employed in grocery stores earned a mean annual salary of $23,640 in 2005.

Depending on the store, designers may be offered sick leave and vacation time, health and life insurance, and other benefits.

WORK ENVIRONMENT

Flowers can be purchased almost anywhere, from small strip-mall flower shops to large national chains to the neighborhood grocery store. This availability means that floral designers can work almost anywhere—from remote, rural areas to busy cities.

Retail floral designers can expect to have comfortable work surroundings. Most floral shops are cool, clean, and well decorated to help attract customers. Glass refrigerators filled with fresh flowers, live plants and flower arrangements, and arts and crafts are typical items in any flower shop. Work stations for making floral pieces are usually found in the back of the store, along with supplies, containers, and necessary equipment.

Expect to spend the majority of the time on your feet—either standing while working on an arrangement, consulting with customers regarding types of flowers, or on a flower-buying expedition. Most retail-based designers work a normal eight-hour workday with a day off during the week. Weekends are especially busy (often because of weddings) and holidays notoriously so. Christmas, Mother's Day, and Valentine's Day are peak times for floral orders. Long work hours are the norm during these times to accommodate the heavy demand for flowers.

Most designers, if contracted to work a wedding, will travel to the church or the banquet hall to make sure the church arrangements or the table arrangements are properly set up.

OUTLOOK

Employment in floral design is expected to grow about as fast as the average for all occupations through 2014, according to the U.S. Department of Labor. At least one flower shop is situated in even the smallest of towns. The emergence of full-service floral departments in grocery stores and opportunities in Internet floral shops have contributed to job availability. Floral experts able to create exciting and original designs will be in high demand. Certified designers may have an edge for the best jobs.

A growing population with large disposable incomes is good news for this industry. Sending flowers to mark an occasion is an old tradition that still has impact today. However, advancement in this career is limited unless you choose to enter management or open a business. Also, starting hourly pay for floral designers is considerably lower than in other design fields.

FOR MORE INFORMATION

For information on classes and schedules, contact
American Floral Art School
634 South Wabash Avenue, Suite 210
Chicago, IL 60605-1808
Tel: 312-922-9328
http://www.americanfloralartschool.com

For information on student chapters and scholarships available through the AIFD Foundation, contact
American Institute of Floral Designers (AIFD)
720 Light Street
Baltimore, MD 21230-3850
Tel: 410-752-3318
Email: AIFD@assnhqtrs.com
http://www.aifd.org

Contact the Rittners School of Floral Design for career and education information. You can also visit its Web site for information on classes and information on how to care for and arrange floral materials.
Rittners School of Floral Design
345 Marlborough Street
Boston, MA 02115-1713
Tel: 617-267-3824
Email: Stevrt@tiac.net
http://www.floralschool.com

For education information, including online courses offered through the SAF, contact
Society of American Florists (SAF)
1601 Duke Street
Alexandria, VA 22314-3406
Tel: 703-836-8700
Email: info@safnow.org
http://www.safnow.org

For fun and interesting information about flowers, visit the SAF's Aboutflowers.com Web site.
Aboutflowers.com
http://www.aboutflowers.com

━━━━━━━━━ **INTERVIEW** ━━━━━━━━━

W. Ian Whipple is a floral designer and the publisher of the magazine *Florist and Grower*. He resides in Idaho Falls, Idaho. Ian discussed his career with the editors of *Careers in Focus: Retail*.

Q. **Please tell us about yourself and your business(es), including *Florist and Grower*.**

A. I'm a father of five. We depend on our businesses for our livelihood. As a young child, I had a great interest in plants and in art. My dad taught me to work hard yet discouraged me from seeking an occupation in an "art" field (probably for fear that I would starve). I started my business from my home in 1987. I tried to find a niche that wasn't being serviced.

In 1992, we moved the business from the home to a retail location of 800 square feet. This was a big step. We continued to take reasonable risks.

We currently have a retail location of 4,000 square feet. Over the years our business has experienced periods of rapid growth. For several years our sales doubled. Our organizational systems have always tried to keep up with the growth. We've always felt undercapitalized. We've developed strict operational budgets out of necessity in order to survive an ever changing industry. We've grown stronger.

In 2004, we opened a design studio in Jackson Hole, Wyoming, and I became the contract florist at a Four Seasons Resort. This has given me great opportunities to use my design experience and expertise in servicing high-end clients. I've always felt that education is important in our industry. I seek out educational opportunities. I try to stay on top of the industry. I have an open mind to new product, new methods, and new ideas.

In May of this year I became the publisher of *Florist and Grower*. I saw it as a tool to bring education and ideas to those in our industry. I've tried over the past few months to improve the quality of the publication, increase the educational value, and strengthen the advertising support.

Q. **Please briefly describe your primary and secondary job responsibilities.**

A. My primary responsibilities are creative director for the retail shop, contract designer at the Four Seasons, and publisher of *Florist and Grower.* I try to inspire, encourage, and educate my staff to excel in their positions. I inspire hotel patrons with beautiful "floral art." I also educate and distribute information through *Florist and Grower.*

Q. How did you train for this job? What was your college major or did you train in another way?

A. The art background came at a very young age. My mother is an artist and taught all her children to be creative. My grandmother taught me to love gardening and plants. The floral industry is a combination of art and nature. I obtained an associate's degree in floral design management from Ricks College (now Brigham Young University-Idaho) in Rexburg, Idaho. My best knowledge and experience has come through professional associations, others in the industry, and work experience. In 2003, I participated in the Accreditation Evaluation Session for the American Institute of Floral Designers (AIFD), the most prestigious national accreditation for florists. I passed and was inducted in 2004 at the National Symposium in New York City. AIFD has been a great source for education, networking, and inspiration. [For more information on AIFD, visit http://www.aifd.org.]

Q.What are the most important personal and professional qualities for people in your career?

A. Most florists are artists and their medium is flowers. Yet, the floral industry is often not taken seriously as a business. Many designers lack a strong business background and business sense. Thus, long-term survival becomes difficult. Strong computer, communication, and organization skills are very important. If the designer doesn't have them, then he needs to work with someone who does.

Q. What are some of the pros and cons of your job?

A. I enjoy what I do. My profession affects the lives of many people in a positive way. I have some flexibility in my daily schedule. I can work from home at times. I can provide for the needs of my family.

Earlier in my career, I felt limited by the amount of monetary compensation offered in the industry. Holidays are usually spent filling orders for customers.

Q. What advice would you give to young people who are interested in the field?

A. Develop strong business skills. Define your niche. Set goals. Be persistent. Be a creative problem solver. Continually seek educational opportunities.

Franchise Owners

OVERVIEW

A *franchise owner* contracts with a company to sell that company's products or services. After paying an initial fee and agreeing to pay the company a certain percentage of revenue, the franchise owner can use the company's name, logo, and guidance. McDonald's, Subway, and KFC are some of the top franchised companies that have locations all across the country. Franchises, however, are not limited to the fast-food industry. Today, franchises are available in a wide variety of business areas, including computer service, lawn care, real estate, and even hair salons. According to the International Franchise Association (IFA), franchises account for nearly 50 percent of all retail sales in the United States, and these sales total more than $1.5 trillion a year.

HISTORY

Know anybody with an antique Singer sewing machine? Chances are, it was originally sold by one of the first franchise operations. During the Civil War, the Singer Sewing Machine Company recognized the cost efficiency of franchising and allowed dealers across the country to sell its sewing machines. Coca-Cola, as well as the Ford Motor Company and other automobile manufacturers, followed Singer's lead in the early 20th century by granting individuals the rights to sell their products. Franchising, however, didn't fully catch on until after World War II, when the needs for products and services across the country boomed, right along with the population. Ray Kroc jumped on the bandwagon with his McDonald's restaurants in the

1950s. Since then, the McDonald's franchise has become one of the top money-making franchise opportunities of all time.

Franchises have changed somewhat over the last 20 to 30 years. Abuses of the franchise system brought new government regulations in the 1970s, and the government has been actively involved in protecting the rights of both franchisers and franchisees. Also, single-unit ownership (the "mom and pop" operation) is giving way to multiple-unit ownership; a majority of franchisees now own more than one of the franchiser's units.

THE JOB

Today, industry experts report that franchises are responsible for nearly 50 percent of all retail sales in the United States, and this figure is expected to grow through the 21st century. *Franchisers* (those companies that sell franchise businesses) and *franchisees* (those who buy the businesses) are sharing in the more than $1.5 trillion a year that franchise businesses take in. While everyone probably has a favorite business or two—maybe the neighborhood Krispy Kreme, with its fresh crullers, or the 7-11 down the street, with its gallon-sized sodas—not everyone may realize that these are franchised establishments. For those interested in starting their own businesses, becoming franchisees may offer just the right mix of risk and security. Any new business venture comes with a certain amount of risk, but franchises offer new owners the security of a name and product that customers are used to and are willing to seek out. Someone with money to invest, the willingness to work hard and sometimes long hours, and the desire to operate a retail business may be able to become the successful franchisee, sharing in the franchiser's success.

There's a franchise for practically every type of product and service imaginable. In addition to the familiar McDonald's and Burger King, other franchise operations exist: businesses that offer temporary employment services, maid services, weight control centers, and custom picture framing, to name a few. The IFA, in fact, reports that approximately 75 different industries make use of the franchise system. No matter what business a person is interested in, there are probably franchise opportunities available.

Depending on the size and nature of the franchise, owners' responsibilities will differ. Those who are able to make a large initial investment may also be able to hire managers and staff members to assist them. Those running a smaller business will need to handle most, if not all, of the job responsibilities themselves.

Though there should be assistance from the franchiser in terms of training, marketing guidance, and established business systems, the business is essentially the franchisee's own. The franchisee pays an initial franchise fee, makes royalty payments to the franchiser, purchases equipment, and rents business space. Any franchisee must handle administrative details such as recordkeeping, creating budgets, and preparing reports for the franchiser. A franchisee is also responsible for hiring (and firing) employees, scheduling work hours, preparing payroll, and keeping track of inventory. Using the franchiser's marketing methods, the franchisee advertises the business. The practices and systems of franchisers differ, so those interested in this work need to carefully research the franchise before buying into it.

Some owners work directly with the clientele. Of course, someone who owns multiple units of the McDonald's franchise probably won't be taking orders at the counter; but someone who owns a single unit of a smaller operation, like a pool maintenance service, may be actively involved in the work at hand, in dealing with customers, and in finding new customers.

Donna Weber of Redmond, Washington, owns a Jazzercise franchise. Jazzercise is the world's largest dance fitness franchise corporation, with more than 6,300 instructors leading 20,000 classes weekly. "I own and teach seven Jazzercise classes a week in two suburbs around the Seattle area," Weber says. After investing with an initial low franchise fee, Weber went through considerable training and testing; the training involves instruction on exercise physiology, dance/exercise technique, and safety issues, as well as instruction on the business aspect of owning a franchise. After training, Weber received certification and started her business. She pays a monthly fee to Jazzercise and in return receives choreography notes to new songs and videos demonstrating the exercises.

In addition to conducting classes, Weber spends some part of every workday preparing paperwork for the corporate headquarters. "I keep track of my students' attendance and write personal postcards to those I haven't seen in a while, those who are having birthdays, those who need some personal recognition for a job well done, etc.," says Weber, who must also regularly learn new routines. "I teach three different formats," she says, "regular aerobics, step, and a circuit-training class each week, so there is a lot of prep to do a good, safe class."

The franchisee's experience will be affected by the name recognition of the business. If it's a fairly new business, the franchisee may have to take on much of the responsibility of promoting it. If it is a well-established business, however, customers and clients already know what to expect from the operation.

REQUIREMENTS

High School

Business, math, economics, and accounting courses will be the most valuable to you in preparing for franchise ownership. Before buying into a franchise, you'll have to do a lot of research into the company, analyzing local demographics to determine whether a business is a sound investment. English classes will help you develop the research skills you'll need. In addition, you will need to hone your communication skills, which will be essential in establishing relationships with franchisers and customers. Take computer classes, since it is virtually impossible to work in today's business world without knowing how to use a computer or the Web. If you already know of a particular area that interests you—such as food service, fashion, or, like Donna Weber, fitness—take classes that will help you learn more about it. Such classes may include home economics, art, dance, or physical education.

Postsecondary Training

Because so many franchise opportunities are available, there is no single educational path for everyone to take on the road to owning a franchise. Keep in mind, however, that when franchisers review your application for the right to purchase a unit, they'll take into consideration your experience in the area. Obviously, a real estate company is unlikely to take a risk on you if you've never had any experience as a broker. In addition, some franchise opportunities require degrees; for example, to own an environmental consulting agency, a business which helps companies meet government environmental standards, you'll have to be an engineer or geologist. But there are also many companies willing to sell to someone wanting to break into a new business. Franchisers will often include special training as part of the initial franchise fee.

Experts in the field stress the importance of gaining work experience before starting out with your own business. Hone your sales, management, and people skills and take the time to learn about the industry that interests you. Even if you don't plan on getting a college degree, consider taking some college-level courses in subjects such as business and finance. One recent survey of franchisees found that over 80 percent had attended college or had a college degree. This reflects the fact that many franchisees have worked for many years in other professions in order to have the money and security needed for starting new businesses. Some organizations and schools, for example, the Schulze School of Entrepreneurship at the University of St. Thomas (http://www.stthomas.edu/cob/schoolofentrepreneurship/default.html) offer courses for prospective franchisees.

Certification or Licensing

Some franchisers have their own certification process and require their franchisees to go through training. You may also want to receive the certification certified franchise executive offered by the Institute of Certified Franchise Executives, an organization affiliated with the IFA. This certification involves completing a certain number of courses in topics such as economics and franchise law, participating in events such as seminars or conventions, and work experience. Although certification is voluntary, it will show your level of education and commitment to the field as well as give you the opportunity to network with other franchise professionals.

You may also need to obtain a small business license to own a franchise unit in your state. Regulations vary depending on the state and the type of business, so it is important that you check with your state's licensing board for specifics before you invest in a franchise.

Other Requirements

As with any small business, you need self-motivation and discipline in order to make your franchise unit successful. Though you'll have some help from your franchiser, the responsibilities of ownership are your own. You'll also need a good credit rating to be eligible for a bank loan, or you'll need enough money of your own for the initial investment. You should be fairly cautious—many people are taken every year in fraudulent franchise schemes. But at the same time, you should feel comfortable taking some risks.

EXPLORING

One relatively easy way to learn about franchising is to do some research on the Web. The International Franchise Association, for example, hosts a very informative Web site (http://www.franchise. org). The association also offers the magazine *Franchising World*. Also, check out your public library or bookstores for the many business magazines that report on small business opportunities. Many of these magazines, such as *Entrepreneur* (http://www.entrepreneurmag.com), publish special editions dealing specifically with franchises.

Join your high school's business club, a group that may give you the opportunity to meet business leaders in your community.

Top 10 Fastest-Growing Franchises, 2006

1. Subway (fast food)

2. Pizza Hut Inc. (fast food)

3. Quiznos (fast food)

4. Jan-Pro Franchising International (commercial cleaning service)

5. Curves for Women (women's fitness centers)

6. Jani-King (commercial cleaning service)

7. Jackson Hewitt Tax Service

8. The UPS Store (business, communication, and postal service centers)

9. Coverall Cleaning Concepts (commercial cleaning service)

10. CleanNet USA Inc. (commercial cleaning service)

Source: *Entrepreneur*

Find a local franchise owner and ask to meet with him or her for an informational interview. Discuss the pros and cons of franchise ownership, find out about the owner's educational and professional background, and ask him or her for general advice. Also, most franchise companies will send you brochures about their franchise opportunities. Request some information and read about what's involved in owning a franchise unit.

Think about what industry interests you, such as services, fast food, health and fitness, or computers. Come up with your own ideas for a franchise business and do some research to find out if this business already exists. If it does, there may be a part-time or summer job opportunity there for you. If it doesn't, keep the idea in mind for your future, but go ahead and get some work experience now. Many franchises hire high school students, and even if you end up working at a Subway when what you're really interested in is lawn care, you'll still be gaining valuable experience dealing with customers, handling sales, and working with others.

EMPLOYERS

There are a number of franchise directories available that list hundreds of franchise opportunities in diverse areas. While some franchisers sell units all across the country, others do business only in a few states. Some of the most successful franchises can guarantee a franchisee great revenue, but these franchise units can require hundreds of thousands of dollars in initial investment.

Many franchisees own more than one franchise unit with a company; some even tie two different franchises together in a practice called "cross-branding." For example, a franchisee may own a pizza franchise as well as an ice cream franchise housed in the same restaurant. Another combination owners find popular is having a convenience store that also houses a fast-food outlet.

STARTING OUT

Before you invest a cent or sign any papers, you should do extensive research into the franchise, particularly if it's a fairly new company. There are many disreputable franchise operations, so you need to be certain of what you're investing in. Lawyers and franchise consultants offer their services to assist people in choosing franchises; some consultants also conduct seminars. The Federal Trade Commission (FTC) publishes *The FTC Consumer Guide to Buying a Franchise* and other relevant publications. The IFA also provides free franchise-buying advice.

You'll need money for the initial franchise fee and for the expenses of the first few years of business. You may pursue a loan from a bank or from business associates, or you may use your own savings. In some cases your start-up costs will be very low; in others you'll need money for a computer, rental of workspace, equipment, signs, and staff. According to the IFA, total start-up costs can range from $20,000 or less to over $1,000,000, depending on the franchise selected and whether it is necessary to own or lease real estate to operate the business. Moreover, the initial franchise fee for most franchisers is between $20,000 and $28,000.

Some franchises can cost much less. Donna Weber's Jazzercise franchise required an initial $600 franchise fee. Though her business has been successful, she must share her gross income. "Twenty percent of that goes back to Jazzercise each month as a fee, I pay about 23 percent of the gross for monthly rent, and 8.6 percent to the state of Washington for sales tax collected on the price of my tickets. There are lots of women grossing $75,000 a year doing this, and there are some who choose to do this for fun and make nothing in return. It's all in how you make it work for you."

ADVANCEMENT

A new franchise unit usually takes a few years to turn profitable. Once the business has proven a success, franchisees may choose to invest in other franchise units with the same company. Franchise owners may also be able to afford to hire management and other staff to take on some of the many responsibilities of the business.

EARNINGS

The earnings for franchisees vary greatly depending on such factors as the type of franchise they own, the amount of money a franchisee was able to initially invest without taking a loan, the franchise's location, and the number of franchise units the franchisee owns. An International Franchise Association survey of 1,000 franchise owners found that the average yearly salary of this group was $91,630. Approximately 24 percent earned more than $100,000 annually.

Since franchisees run their own businesses, they generally do not have paid sick days or holidays. In addition, they are typically responsible for providing their own insurance and retirement plans.

WORK ENVIRONMENT

Owning a franchise unit can be demanding, requiring work of 60 to 70 hours a week, but owners have the satisfaction of knowing that their business's success is a result of their own hard work. Some people look for franchise opportunities that are less demanding and may only require a part-time commitment. "I'm not getting rich," Donna Weber says, "but I love my job, and I love being my own boss. I can schedule my vacations when I want; we usually don't close our classes down, so we hire certified Jazzercise substitutes."

Franchise owners who handle all the business details personally may consider this work to be very stressful. In addition, dealing with the hiring, management, and sometimes firing of staff can be difficult. In some situations, much of a franchisee's work will be limited to an office setting; in other situations, such as with a home inspection service or a maid service, the franchisee drives to remote sites to work with clients. Some franchises are mobile in nature, and these will involve a lot of traveling within a designated region.

OUTLOOK

While some experts say that the success rate of franchises is very high and a great deal of money can be made with a franchise unit, others say franchising isn't as successful as starting an independent business. According to the U.S. Department of Commerce, less than five percent of franchised outlets have failed each year since 1971. However, when reporting figures, franchisers don't always consider a unit as failing if it is under different ownership but still in operation. The employment outlook will depend on factors such as the economy—a downturn in the economy is always most difficult for new businesses—as well as the type of franchise. Overall, though, growth should be steady and about as fast as the average.

FOR MORE INFORMATION

For information about buying a franchise and a list of AAFD-accredited franchisers, contact
American Association of Franchisees & Dealers (AAFD)
PO Box 81887
San Diego, CA 92138-1887
Tel: 800-733-9858
Email: Benefits@aafd.org
http://www.aafd.org

Visit the FTC's Web site for information on franchising, including the publication A Consumer Guide to Buying a Franchise.
Federal Trade Commission (FTC)
600 Pennsylvania Avenue NW
Washington, DC 20580-0001
Tel: 202-326-2222
http://www.ftc.gov

For more information on franchising as well as a free newsletter, contact
FranchiseHelp
101 Executive Boulevard, 2nd Floor
Elmsford, NY 10523-1316
Tel: 800-401-1446
Email: company@franchisehelp.com
http://www.franchisehelp.com

For general information about franchising, specific franchise opportunities, and publications, contact the IFA
International Franchise Association (IFA)
1501 K Street NW, Suite 350
Washington, DC 20005-1412
Tel: 202-628-8000
Email: ifa@franchise.org
http://www.franchise.org

INTERVIEW

Steve and Janine Zulanas have owned a pizza franchise in Colorado for almost five years. They discussed their careers with the editors of *Careers in Focus: Retail*.

Q. What made you want to become franchise owners?

A. We opened up this pizza place as an investment as well as to provide a service to a community that had a high demand for GREAT pizza.

Q. Please briefly describe your job responsibilities as franchise owners.

A. Our responsibility as franchise owners it to provide a quality of pizza that people expect with the franchise's name. Consistency is an important factor when comparing us to our competitors. Our second goal is to please our customers one order at a time!

Q. What are the most important personal and professional qualities for franchise owners?

A. As an owner, you need to make sure you put 110 percent into your business. You have to be committed and believe in your product. As a professional, you need a staff that you can trust and feel confident that they will get all the jobs done.

Q. What are some of the pros and cons of your job?

A. Pros: seeing the success, making people happy, taking control of your professional life. Cons: tons of hours, hiring entry-level people, firing people, the everyday highs and lows.

Q. What advice would you give to young people who are interested in becoming franchise owners?

A. Do your homework, research, and make sure it's what you want to do. The first couple of years you "eat, drink, and sleep" your business. Make sure you have the financial support, and make sure you have strong, trustworthy people working for you.

Internet Store Managers and Entrepreneurs

OVERVIEW

Internet store managers and entrepreneurs use the exciting technology of the Internet to sell products or services. They may research the marketability of a product or service, decide on what product or service to sell, organize their business, and set up their storefront on the Web. Numerous small business owners who sell a limited number of products or a specific service have found the Internet a great place to begin their business venture because start-up costs may be less than for traditional businesses. Internet entrepreneurs run their own businesses. Internet store managers are employed by Internet entrepreneurs and stores.

HISTORY

The Internet became a popular sales tool in the 1990s, and continues to grow today. Although many dot-com companies failed in the early 2000s, Internet sales remain an integral part of our economy. The career of online sales manager has been listed in *U.S. News & World Report*'s Top 20 Hot Job Tracks.

   In 2002, lawmakers and tax officials from 30 states agreed to enter a voluntary pact to collect online sales tax. According to *Washingtonpost*.com, this action was taken partially in response to regular "bricks-and-mortar" stores who complained that online retailers had an advantage.

More and more revenue is generated online each year, and some Internet stores, such as Amazon.com, have had tremendous success in this field. As the Internet continues to grow in popularity and importance, more consumers will be exposed to Internet stores on a daily basis. This will create a strong demand for Internet managers and entrepreneurs to research and market potential products and services, as well as manage businesses and employees.

THE JOB

In spite of the failure of many high-profile dot-coms in the early 2000s, many online businesses have continued to survive and thrive. These e-tailers have adapted to the constantly changing technology, economic climate, business trends, and consumer demands, instead of concentrating on fast growth and offering the lowest prices. Reports by research firm Jupiter Communications show that consumers are using Internet stores to do comparison shopping, and a significant number of consumers research products online before buying them at traditional stores.

Because of the vastness of the Internet, the role of an Internet store manager or entrepreneur can vary as much as the numerous Web sites on the Internet. Expert opinion on what makes one Web site or one business more successful than another differs, too. E-commerce is a new and relatively unexplored field for entrepreneurs. But, because most entrepreneurs have innovative and creative natures, this uncertainty and uncharted territory is what they love.

Like traditional entrepreneurs, Internet entrepreneurs must have strong business skills. They come up with ideas for an Internet product or service, research the feasibility of selling this product or service, decide what they need to charge to make a profit, determine how to advertise their business, and even arrange for financing for their business if necessary. In addition, Internet entrepreneurs typically have computer savvy and may even create and maintain their own sites.

Some entrepreneurs may choose to market a service, such as Web site design, to target the business-to-business market. Other Internet entrepreneurs may decide to market a service, such as computer dating, to target the individual consumer market. Still others may develop a "virtual store" on the Internet and sell products that target businesses or individual consumers.

Internet stores vary in size, items for sale, and the range of products. Smaller Internet stores, for example, may market the work done by a single craftsperson or businessperson. Many large Internet stores focus on selling a specific product or line of products. As some of these stores have grown they have diversified their merchandise. Amazon.com is one such example. Originally a small, online bookstore, the company now sells music CDs, videos, jewelry, toys and housewares, along with books. Other Internet stores, such as those of Eddie Bauer and Sears, may be extensions of catalog or traditional brick-and-mortar stores. These large companies are generally so well established that they can employ Internet store managers to oversee the virtual store.

Many Internet businesses begin small, with one person working as the owner, manager, Webmaster, marketing director, and accountant, among other positions. John Axne of Chicago, Illinois, took on all these responsibilities when he developed his own one-person business designing Web sites for small companies and corporations. "Having my own business allows me more creative freedom," says Axne. The successful Internet entrepreneur, like the successful traditional entrepreneur, is often able to combine his or her interests with work to fill a niche in the business world. "It's a great fit for me," Axne explains. "I have a passion for computers and a love of learning. This business allows me to sell myself and my services." Dave Wright of Venice, California, is also an Internet entrepreneur and Web site designer. He, too, combined his interests with computer skills to start his business. "I had a strong interest in art," he says. "I simply married my art and graphic art experience with computers."

Those who want to start their own businesses on the Web must be very focused and self-motivated. Just like any other entrepreneur, they always need to keep an eye on the competition to see what products and services as well as prices and delivery times others offer. While Internet entrepreneurs do not need to be computer whizzes, they should enjoy learning about technology so that they can keep up with new developments that may help them with their businesses. Internet entrepreneurs must also be decision makers, and many are drawn to running their own businesses because of the control it offers. "I'm a control freak," Wright admits. "This way I can oversee every aspect of my job."

The typical day of the Internet store manager or entrepreneur will depend greatly on the company he or she works for. Someone who works for a large company that also has a Web site store, for example, may meet with company department heads to find out about upcoming sales or products that should be heavily advertised on the Web site. They may do research about the store use and report their findings to company managers. They may work on the site itself, updating it with new information.

The Internet entrepreneur also has varied responsibilities that depend on his or her business. Wright notes, "No two projects and no two days are alike." An entrepreneur may spend one day working with a client to determine the client's needs and the next day working on bookkeeping and advertising in addition to working on a project. Most entrepreneurs, however, enjoy this variety and flexibility.

While the Internet world is appealing to many, there are risks for those who start their own businesses. "The Internet changes so rapidly that in five years it may be entirely different," Wright says. "That's why I started a business that simply sells services and didn't require a major investment. It is a business that I can get into and out of quickly if I find it necessary. There is no product, per se, and no inventory." Despite uncertainties, however, Web stores continue to open and the number of Internet store managers and entrepreneurs continues to grow.

REQUIREMENTS

High School

If you are considering becoming an Internet store manager or entrepreneur, there are a number of classes you can take in high school to help prepare you for these careers. Naturally, you should take computer science courses to give you a familiarity with using computers and the Web. Business and marketing courses will also be beneficial for you. Also, take mathematics, accounting, or bookkeeping classes because, as an entrepreneur, you will be responsible for your company's finances. Take history classes to learn about economic trends and psychology classes to learn about human behavior. A lot of advertising and product promotion has a psychological element. Finally, take plenty of English classes. These classes will help you develop your communication skills—skills that will be vital to your work as a store manager or business owner.

Postsecondary Training

Although there are no specific educational requirements for Internet store managers or entrepreneurs, a college education will certainly enhance your skills and chances for success. Like anyone interested in working for or running a traditional business, take plenty of business, economics, and marketing and management classes. Your education should also include accounting or bookkeeping classes. Keep up with computer and Internet developments by taking computer classes. Some schools offer certificates and degrees in e-commerce. Many schools have undergraduate degree programs in business or business administration, but you can also enter this field with other degrees. Dave Wright, for example, graduated with a degree from art school, while John Axne has degrees in biomedical engineering and interactive media.

Certification or Licensing

While no specific certifications are available for Internet store managers and entrepreneurs, professional associations such as the Institute for Certification of Computing Professionals and the Institute of Certified Professional Managers offer voluntary management-related certifications to industry professionals. These designations are helpful in proving your abilities to an employer. The more certifications you have, the more you have to offer.

Licenses may be required for running a business, depending on the type of business. Since requirements vary, you will need to check with local and state agencies for regulations in your area.

Other Requirements

Internet entrepreneurs and store managers must have the desire and initiative to keep up on new technology and business trends. Because they must deal with many different people in various lines of work, they need to be flexible problem solvers and have strong communication skills. Creativity and insight into new and different ways of doing business are qualities that are essential for an entrepreneur to be successful. In addition, because the Internet and e-commerce are relatively new and the future of Internet businesses is uncertain, those who enter the field are generally risk-takers and eager to be on the cutting edge of commerce and technology. Dave Wright notes, "This is not a job for someone looking for security. The Internet world is always changing. This is both exciting and scary to me as a businessperson. This is one career where you are not able to see where you will be in five years."

EXPLORING

There are numerous ways in which you can explore your interest in the computer and business worlds. Increase your computer skills and find out how much this technology interests you by joining a computer users group or club at your high school or your community. Access the Internet frequently on your own to observe different Web site designs and find out what is being sold and marketed electronically. What sites do you think are best at promoting products and why? Think about things from a customer's point of view.

How easy are the sites to access and use? How are the products displayed and accessed? How competitive are the prices for goods or services?

Make it a goal to come up with your own ideas for a product or service to market on the Web, then do some research. How difficult would it be to deliver the product? What type of financing would be involved? Are other sites already providing this product or service? How could you make your business unique?

Talk to professionals in your community about their work. Set up informational interviews with local business owners to find out what is involved in starting and running a traditional business. Your local chamber of commerce or the Small Business Administration may have classes or publications that would help you learn about starting a business. In addition, set up informational interviews with computer consultants, Web site designers, or Internet store managers or owners. How did they get started? What advice do they have? Is there anything they wish they had done differently? Where do they see the future of e-commerce going?

If your school has a future business owners club, join this group to meet others with similar interests. For hands-on business experience, get a part-time or summer job at any type of store in your area. This work will give you the opportunity to deal with customers (who can sometimes be hard to please), work with handling money, and observe how the store promotes its products and services.

EMPLOYERS

Internet store managers may work for an established traditional business or institution that also has a Web site dealing with products and services. The manager may also work for a business that only has a presence on the Web or for an Internet entrepreneur. Entrepreneurs are self-employed, and sometimes they may employ people to work under them. Some Internet entrepreneurs may be hired to begin a business for someone else.

STARTING OUT

Professionals in the field advise those just starting out to work for someone else to gain experience in the business world before beginning their own business. The Internet is a good resource to use to find employment. Many sites post job openings. Local employment agencies and newspapers and trade magazines also list job opportunities. In addition, your college career services office should be able to provide you with help locating a job. Networking with college alumni and people in your computer users groups may also provide job leads.

ADVANCEMENT

Advancement opportunities depend on the business, its success, and the individual's goals. Internet entrepreneurs or store managers who are successful may enter other business fields or consulting. Or they may advance to higher-level management positions or other larger Internet-based businesses. Some entrepreneurs establish a business and then sell it only to begin another business venture. The Internet world is constantly changing because of technological advancements. This state of flux means that a wide variety of possibilities are available to those working in the field. "There is no solid career path in the Internet field," says Dave Wright. "Your next career may not even be developed yet."

EARNINGS

Income for Internet store managers and entrepreneurs is usually tied to the profitability of the business. Internet store managers who work for established traditional businesses are typically salaried employees of the company. Internet entrepreneurs who offer a service may be paid by the project. Entrepreneurs are self-employed and their income will depend on the success of the business. Those just starting out may actually have no earnings, while those with a business that has been existence for several years may have annual earnings between $25,000 and $50,000. Some in the field may earn much more than this amount. John Axne estimates that those who have good technical skills and can do such things as create the database program for a Web site may have higher salaries, in the $60,000 to $125,000 range.

Entrepreneurs are almost always responsible for their own medical, disability, and life insurances. Retirement plans must also be self-funded and self-directed. Internet store managers may or may not receive benefits.

WORK ENVIRONMENT

Internet entrepreneurs and store managers may work out of a home or private office. Some Internet store managers may be required to work on site at a corporation or small business.

The entrepreneur must deal with the stresses of starting a business, keeping it going, dealing with deadlines and customers, and coping with problems as they arise. They must also work long hours to develop and manage their business venture; many entrepreneurs work over 40 hours a week. Evening or weekend work may also be required, both for the entrepreneur and the store manager.

In addition, these professionals must spend time researching, reading, and checking out the competition in order to be informed about the latest technology and business trends. Their intensive computer work can result in eyestrain, hand and wrist injuries, and back pain.

OUTLOOK

Online commerce is a very new and exciting field with tremendous potential, and it is likely that growth will continue over the long term. However, it is important to keep in mind that the failure rate for new businesses, even traditional ones, is fairly high. Some experts predict that in the next few years, 80 to 90 percent of dot-coms will either close or be acquired by other companies. The survivors will be small businesses that are able to find niche markets, anticipate trends, adapt to market and technology changes, and plan for a large enough financial margin to turn a profit. Analysts also anticipate that the amount of business-to-business e-commerce will surpass business-to-consumer sales.

Internet managers and entrepreneurs with the most thorough education and experience and who have done their research will have the best opportunities for success. For those who are adventurous and interested in using new avenues for selling products and services, the Internet offers many possibilities.

FOR MORE INFORMATION

For information about the information technology industry and e-commerce, contact

Information Technology Association of America
1401 Wilson Boulevard, Suite 1100
Arlington, VA 22209-2318
Tel: 703-522-5055
http://www.itaa.org

For certification information, contact

Institute for Certification of Computing Professionals
2350 East Devon Avenue, Suite 115
Des Plaines, IL 60018-4610
Tel: 800-843-8227
http://www.iccp.org

For information on certification, contact
Institute of Certified Professional Managers
James Madison University
MSC 5504
Harrisonburg, VA 22807-0001
Tel: 800-568-4120
Email: icpmcm@jmu.edu
http://cob.jmu.edu/icpm

The Small Business Administration offers helpful information on starting a business. For information on state offices and additional references, visit its Web site.
Small Business Administration
6302 Fairview Road, Suite 300
Charlotte, NC 28210
Tel: 800-827-5722
Email: answerdesk@sba.gov
http://www.sba.gov

Check out the following online magazine specializing in topics of interest to entrepreneurs.
Entrepreneur.com
http://www.entrepreneur.com

Jewelers and Jewelry Repairers

QUICK FACTS

School Subjects
Art
Technical/shop

Personal Skills
Artistic
Mechanical/manipulative

Work Environment
Primarily indoors
Primarily one location

Minimum Education Level
Apprenticeship

Salary Range
$17,590 to $29,430 to
$53,240+

Certification or Licensing
Voluntary

Outlook
Decline

DOT
700

GOE
08.02.02

NOC
7344

O*NET-SOC
51-9071.00, 51-9071.01, 51-
9071.03, 51-9071.04, 51-
9071.05, 51-9071.06

OVERVIEW

Jewelers, sometimes known as bench jewelers, create, either from their own design or one by a design specialist, rings, necklaces, bracelets, and other jewelry out of gold, silver, or platinum. *Jewelry repairers* alter ring sizes, reset stones, and refashion old jewelry. Restringing beads and stones, resetting clasps and hinges, and mending breaks in ceramic and metal pieces also are aspects of jewelry repair. A few jewelers are also trained as *gemologists,* who examine, grade, and evaluate gems, or *gem cutters,* who cut, shape, and polish gemstones. Many jewelers also repair watches and clocks. There are about 42,000 jewelers employed in the United States.

HISTORY

People have always worn adornments of some type. Early cave dwellers fashioned jewelry out of shells or the bones, teeth, or claws of animals. Beads have been found in the graves of prehistoric peoples. During the Iron Age, jewelry was made of ivory, wood, or metal. Precious stones were bought and sold at least 4,000 years ago in ancient Babylon, and there was widespread trade in jewelry by the Phoenicians and others in the Mediterranean and Asia Minor. The ancient Greeks and Romans were particularly fond of gold. Excavations of ancient Egyptian civilization show extremely well crafted jewelry. It was during this time, it is believed, that jewelers first combined gems with precious metals.

Many of the metals jewelers use today, such as gold, silver, copper, brass, and iron, were first discovered or used by ancient jewelers. During the Hashemite Empire, a court jeweler discovered iron while seeking a stronger metal to use in battles. During the Renaissance period in Europe, jewelers became increasingly skillful. Artists such as Botticelli and Cellini used gold and silver with precious stones of every sort to create masterpieces of the gold and silversmiths' trades. Jewelers perfected the art of enameling during this time.

Many skilled artisans brought their trades to Colonial America. The first jewelers were watchmakers, silversmiths, and coppersmiths. In early America, a versatile craft worker might create a ring or repair the copper handle on a cooking pot. By the 1890s, New York City had emerged as a center of the precious metal jewelry industry. It became a center for the diamond trade as well as for other precious stones. The first jewelry store, as we know it today, opened at the turn of the 19th century.

By the early 20th century, machines were used to create jewelry, and manufacturing plants began mass production of costume jewelry. These more affordable items quickly became popular and made jewelry available to large numbers of people.

New York City continues today as a leading center of the precious metals industry and jewelry manufacturing in the United States. Along with Paris and London, New York is a prime location for many fine jewelry designers.

During the 1980s, a small niche of jewelers began creating their own designs and either making them themselves or having other jewelers fabricate them. Also called *jewelry artists,* they differ from more traditional designers both in the designs they create and the methods and materials they use. They sell their designer lines of jewelry in small boutiques, galleries, or at crafts shows or market them to larger retail stores. Many of these jewelers open their own stores. The American Jewelry Design Council was founded in 1990 to help promote designer jewelry as an art form.

THE JOB

Jewelers may design, make, sell, or repair jewelry. Many jewelers combine two or more of these skills. Designers conceive and sketch ideas for jewelry that they may make themselves or have made by another craftsperson. The materials used by the jeweler and the jewelry repairer may be precious, semiprecious, or synthetic. They work with valuable stones such as diamonds and rubies, and precious metals such as gold, silver, and platinum. Some jewelers use synthetic stones in their jewelry to make items more affordable.

The jeweler begins by forming an item in wax or metal with carving tools. The jeweler then places the wax model in a casting ring and pours plaster into the ring to form a mold. The mold is inserted into a furnace to melt the wax and a metal model is cast from the plaster mold. The jeweler pours the precious molten metal into the mold or uses a centrifugal casting machine to cast the article. Cutting, filing, and polishing are final touches the jeweler makes to a piece.

Jewelers do most of their work sitting down. They use small hand and machine tools such as drills, files, saws, soldering irons, and jewelers' lathes. They often wear an eye loupe or magnifying glass. They constantly use their hands and eyes and need good finger and hand dexterity.

Most jewelers specialize in creating certain kinds of jewelry or focus on a particular operation, such as making, polishing, or stone-setting models and tools. Specialists include gem cutters; stone setters; fancy-wire drawers; locket, ring, and hand chain makers; and sample makers.

Silversmiths design, assemble, decorate, or repair silver articles. They may specialize in one or more areas of the jewelry field such as repairing, selling, or appraising. *Jewelry engravers* carve text or graphic decorations on jewelry. *Watchmakers* repair, clean, and adjust mechanisms of watches and clocks.

Gem and diamond workers select, cut, shape, polish, or drill gems and diamonds using measuring instruments, machines, or hand tools. Some work as diamond die polishers, while others are gem cutters.

Other jewelry workers perform such operations as precision casting and modeling of molds, or setting precious and semiprecious stones for jewelry. They may make gold or silver chains and cut designs or lines in jewelry using hand tools or cutting machines. Other jewelers work as pearl restorers or jewelry bench hands.

Assembly line methods are used to produce costume jewelry and some types of precious jewelry, but the models and tools needed for factory production must be made by highly skilled jewelers. Some molds and models for manufacturing are designed and created using computer-aided design/manufacturing systems. Costume jewelry often is made by a die stamping process. In general, the more precious the metals, the less automated the manufacturing process.

Some jewelers and jewelry repairers are self-employed; others work for manufacturing and retail establishments. Workers in a manufacturing plant include skilled, semiskilled, and unskilled positions. Skilled positions include jewelers, ring makers, engravers, toolmakers, electroplaters, and stone cutters and setters. Semiskilled positions include polishers, repairers, toolsetters, and solderers. Unskilled workers are press operators, carders, and linkers.

Although some jewelers operate their own retail stores, an increasing number of jewelry stores are owned or managed by individuals who are not jewelers. In such instances, a jeweler or jewelry repairer may be employed by the owner, or the store may send its repairs to a trade shop operated by a jeweler who specializes in repair work. Jewelers who operate their own stores sell jewelry, watches, and, frequently, merchandise such as silverware, china, and glassware. Many retail jewelry stores are located in or near large cities, with the eastern section of the country providing most of the employment in jewelry manufacturing.

Other jobs in the jewelry business include *appraisers*, who examine jewelry and determine its value and quality; *sales staff*, who set up and care for jewelry displays, take inventory, and help customers; and *buyers*, who purchase jewelry, gems, and watches from wholesalers and resell the items to the public in retail stores.

REQUIREMENTS

High School
A high school education usually is necessary for those desiring to enter the jewelry trade. While you are in high school, take courses in chemistry, physics, mechanical drawing, and art. Computer-aided design classes will be especially beneficial to you if you are planning to design jewelry. Sculpture and metalworking classes will prepare you for design and repair work.

Postsecondary Training
A large number of educational and training programs are available in jewelry and jewelry repair. Trade schools and community colleges offer a variety of programs, including classes in basic jewelry-making skills, techniques, use and care of tools and machines, stone setting, casting, polishing, and gem identification. Programs usually run from six months to one year, although individual classes are shorter and can be taken without enrolling in an entire program.

Some colleges and universities offer programs in jewelry store management, metalwork, and jewelry design. You can also find classes at fashion institutes, art schools, and art museums. In addition, you can take correspondence courses and continuing education classes. For sales and managerial positions in a retail store, college experience is usually helpful. Recommended classes are sales techniques, gemology, advertising, accounting, business administration, and computers.

The work of the jeweler and jewelry repairer may also be learned through an apprenticeship or by informal on-the-job training. The latter often includes instruction in design, quality of precious stones, and chemistry of metals. The apprentice becomes a jeweler upon the successful completion of a two-year apprenticeship and passing written and oral tests covering the trade. The apprenticeship generally focuses on casting, stone setting, and engraving.

Most jobs in manufacturing require on-the-job training, although many employers prefer to hire individuals who have completed a technical education program.

Certification or Licensing

Certification is available in several areas through the Jewelers of America, a trade organization. Those who do bench work (the hands-on work creating and repairing jewelry) can be certified at one of four levels: certified bench jeweler technician, certified bench jeweler, certified senior bench jeweler, and certified master bench jeweler. Each certification involves passing a written test and a bench test. Jewelers of America also offers certification for management and sales workers. Although voluntary, these certifications show that a professional has met certain standards for the field and is committed to this work.

Other Requirements

Jewelers and jewelry repairers need to have extreme patience and skill to handle the expensive materials of the trade. Although the physically disabled may find employment in this field, superior hand-eye coordination is essential. Basic mechanical skills such as filing, sawing, and drilling are vital to the jewelry repairer. Jewelers who work from their own designs need creative and artistic ability. They also should have a strong understanding of metals and their properties. Retail jewelers and those who operate or own trade shops and manufacturing establishments must work well with people and have knowledge of merchandising and business management and practices. Sales staff should be knowledgeable and friendly, and buyers must have good judgment, self-confidence, and leadership abilities. Because of the expensive nature of jewelry, some people working in the retail industry are bonded, which means they must pass the requirements for an insurance company to underwrite them.

EXPLORING

If you are interested in becoming a jeweler or jewelry repairer, you can become involved in arts and crafts activities and take classes in crafts and jewelry making. Many community education programs are available through high schools, park districts, or local art stores and museums. Hobbies such as metalworking and sculpture are useful in becoming familiar with metals and the tools jewelers use. Visits to museums and fine jewelry stores to see collections of jewelry can be helpful.

If you are interested in the retail aspect of this field, you should try to find work in a retail jewelry store on a part-time basis or during the summer. A job in sales, or even as a clerk, can provide a firsthand introduction to the business. A retail job will help you become familiar with a jewelry store's operations, its customers, and the jewelry sold. In addition, you will learn the terminology unique to the jewelry field. Working in a store with an in-house jeweler or jewelry repairer provides many opportunities to observe and speak with a professional engaged in this trade. In a summer or part-time job as a bench worker or assembly line worker in a factory, you may perform only a few of the operations involved in making jewelry, but you will be exposed to many of the skills used within a manufacturing plant.

You also may want to visit retail stores and shops where jewelry is made and repaired or visit a jewelry factory. Some boutiques and galleries are owned and operated by jewelers who enjoy the opportunity to talk to people about their trade. Art fairs and craft shows where jewelers exhibit and sell their products provide a more relaxed environment where jewelers are likely to have time to discuss their work.

EMPLOYERS

Approximately 42,000 jewelers and precious stone and metal workers are employed in the United States. Jewelers work in a variety of settings, from production work in multinational corporations to jewelry stores and repair shops. Some jewelers specialize in gem and diamond work, watchmaking, jewelry appraisal, repair, or engraving, where they may work in manufacturing or at the retail level. Other jewelers work only as appraisers. In most cases, appraisals are done by store owners or jewelers who have years of experience. About 40 percent of all jewelers are self-employed. Most self-employed jewelers own their own stores or repair shops or specialize in designing and creating custom jewelry. Top states for jewelry manufacturing include Rhode Island, New York, and California.

STARTING OUT

A summer or part-time job in a jewelry store or the jewelry department of a department store will help you learn about the business. Another way to enter this line of work is to contact jewelry manufacturing establishments in major production centers. A trainee can acquire the many skills needed in the jewelry trade. The number of trainees accepted in this manner, however, is relatively small. Students who have completed a training program improve their chances of finding work as an apprentice or trainee. Students may learn about available jobs and apprenticeships through the career services offices of training schools they attend, from local jewelers, or from the personnel offices of manufacturing plants.

Those desiring to establish their own retail businesses find it helpful to first obtain employment with an established jeweler or a manufacturing plant. Considerable financial investment is required to open a retail jewelry store, and jewelers in such establishments find it to their advantage to be able to do repair work on watches as well as the usual jeweler's work. Less financial investment is needed to open a trade shop. These shops generally tend to be more successful in or near areas with large populations where they can take advantage of the large volume of jewelry business. Both retail jewelry stores and trade shops are required to meet local and state business laws and regulations.

ADVANCEMENT

There are many opportunities for advancement in the jewelry field. Jewelers and jewelry repairers can go into business for themselves once they have mastered the skills of their trade. They may create their own designer lines of jewelry that they market and sell, or they can open a trade shop or retail store. Many self-employed jewelers gain immense satisfaction from the opportunity to specialize in one aspect of jewelry or to experiment with new methods and materials.

Workers in jewelry manufacturing have fewer opportunities for advancement than in other areas of jewelry because of the declining number of workers needed. Plant workers in semiskilled and unskilled positions can advance based on the speed and quality of their work and by perseverance. On-the-job training can provide opportunities for higher-skilled positions. Workers in manufacturing who show proficiency can advance to supervisory and management positions or may leave manufacturing and go to work in a retail shop or trade shop.

The most usual avenue of advancement is from employee in a factory, shop, or store to owner or manager of a trade shop or retail store. Sales is an excellent starting place for people who want to own their own store. Sales staff receive firsthand training in customer relations as well as knowledge of the different aspects of jewelry store merchandising. Sales staff may become gem experts who are qualified to manage a store, and managers may expand their territory from one store to managing several stores in a district or region. Top management in retail offers many interesting and rewarding positions to people who are knowledgeable, responsible, and ambitious. Buyers may advance by dealing exclusively with fine gems that are more expensive, and some buyers become *diamond merchants,* buying diamonds on the international market.

Jewelry designers' success depends not only on the skill with which they make jewelry but also on their ability to create new designs and keep in touch with current trends in the consumer market. Jewelry designers attend craft shows, trade shows, and jewelry exhibitions to see what others are making and to get ideas for new lines of jewelry.

EARNINGS

Jewelers and precious stone and metal workers had median annual earnings of $29,430 in 2005, according to the U.S. Department of Labor. Salaries ranged from less than $17,590 to more than $53,240. Most jewelers start out with a base salary. With experience, they can charge by the number of pieces completed. Jewelers who work in retail stores may earn a commission for each piece of jewelry sold, in addition to their base salary.

Most employers offer benefit packages that include paid holidays and vacations and health insurance. Retail stores may offer discounts on store purchases.

WORK ENVIRONMENT

Jewelers work in a variety of environments. Some self-employed jewelers design and create jewelry in their homes; others work in small studios or trade shops. Jewelers who create their own designer lines of jewelry may travel to retail stores and other sites to promote their merchandise. Many designers also attend trade shows and exhibitions to learn more about current trends. Some sell their jewelry at both indoor and outdoor art shows and craft fairs. These shows are held on weekends, evenings, or during the week. Many jewelry artists live and work near tourist areas or in art communities.

Workers in jewelry manufacturing plants usually work in clean, air-conditioned, and relatively quiet environments. Workers in departments such as polishing, electroplating, and lacquer spraying may be exposed to fumes from chemicals and solvents. Workers who do bench work sit at workstations. Other workers stand at an assembly line for many hours at a time. Many workers in a manufacturing plant perform only one or two types of operations so the work can become repetitious. Most employees in a manufacturing plant work 35-hour workweeks, with an occasional need for overtime.

Retail store owners, managers, jewelers, and sales staff work a variety of hours and shifts that include weekends, especially during the Christmas season, the busiest time of year. Buyers may work more than 40 hours a week because they must travel to see wholesalers. Work settings vary from small shops and boutiques to large department stores. Most jewelry stores are clean, quiet, pleasant, and attractive. However, most jewelry store employees spend many hours on their feet dealing with customers, and buyers travel a great deal.

OUTLOOK

Employment of jewelers is expected to decline through 2014, according to the *Occupational Outlook Handbook*. Despite this prediction, jewelers and jewelry repairers will continue to be needed to replace those workers who leave the workforce or move to new positions. Since jewelry sales are increasing at rates that exceed the number of new jewelers entering the profession, employers are finding it difficult to find skilled employees.

Consumers now are purchasing jewelry from mass marketers, discount stores, catalogs, television shopping shows, and the Internet as well as from traditional retail stores. This may result in store closings or limited hiring.

The number of workers in manufacturing plants is declining because of increased automation, but opportunities for skilled workers should remain fairly steady. Demand in retail is growing for people who are skilled in personnel, management, sales and promotion, advertising, floor and window display, and buying. Opportunities will be best for graduates of training programs for jewelers or gemologists.

FOR MORE INFORMATION

For information on designer jewelry, contact
> **American Jewelry Design Council**
> 760 Market Street, Suite 900
> San Francisco, CA 94102-2304
> http://www.ajdc.org

For an information packet with tuition prices, application procedures, and course descriptions, contact
> **Gemological Institute of America**
> The Robert Mouawad Campus
> 5345 Armada Drive
> Carlsbad, CA 92008-4602
> Tel: 800-421-7250, ext. 4001 (admissions)
> Email: admissions@gia.edu
> http://www.gia.edu

For certification information, a school directory, and a copy of Careers in the Jewelry Industry, *contact*
> **Jewelers of America**
> 52 Vanderbilt Avenue, 19th Floor
> New York, NY 10017-3827
> Tel: 800-223-0673
> Email: info@jewelers.org
> http://www.jewelers.org

For career and school information, contact
> **Manufacturing Jewelers and Suppliers of America**
> 45 Royal Little Drive
> Providence, RI 02904-1861
> Tel: 800-444-6572
> Email: info@mjsa.org
> http://mjsa.polygon.net

═══ INTERVIEW ═══

Tom Weishaar is a bench jeweler in Fayetteville, Arkansas. He discussed his career with the editors of *Careers in Focus: Retail*.

Q. Please briefly describe your primary and secondary job responsibilities as a bench jeweler.

A. My primary responsibility as a bench jeweler is to organize, maintain, and run a profitable "shop" for the store in which I work. On the surface this doesn't sound odd, but most in-store jewelry shops are not profitable. Many stores use their shops as a loss leader, a means by which to get customers to purchase jewelry. This results in a Catch-22 situation. Store owners won't compensate bench jewelers because of low profit margins from the shop and bench jewelers are in turn less motivated to generate higher profits. The shop I run is profitable, and I am compensated at a much higher rate than the norm.

My secondary job is to work with customers and help explain why their jewelry needs repair and how the repairs will be done. This one-on-one approach helps to break down barriers and elevates the profitability of my shop.

Q. How did you train for this career? Is the training different today from when you started in the field?

A. My training did not follow the normal pattern. I took a degree in art education from Northern Illinois University, with a minor in metal smithing. After graduation there were few teaching positions to be had, so I fell back on my metal smithing abilities and took a job as a bench jeweler. Having the degree gives me great insight into art and the ability to communicate with others. These skills are lacking in the traditional approach for bench jeweler training.

The traditional method of learning to become a bench jeweler is to apprentice to an established bench jeweler. This method has been used for centuries and though it is now rare, it is still in practice. The modern method developed in the past 50 years is to attend a trade school and get a two-year associate's degree in jewelry repair. There are five schools across the country that teach people the basics of becoming bench jewelers.

Q. What are the most important personal and professional qualities for bench jewelers?

A. The most important quality is to treat this career as a profession and not a hobby or craft. By this I mean that bench jewelers need to strive to become better jewelers. You must understand that nearly all bench jewelers work alone. The opportunity to grow and develop one's talents must be self motivated—otherwise stagnation occurs. Few bench jewelers avail themselves of the published materials, which could help them learn new techniques or improve their skills. Even fewer jewelers attend professional seminars presented by their peers or attend continuing educational courses where knowledge can be exchanged. Sadly, most new knowledge comes through experimentation on customer's jewelry.

Q. What are some of the pros and cons of your job?

A. The bench jeweler profession can be wonderful. Jewelers tend to be fussy people who like to tinker and work with their hands. The job is ever changing and challenging. There are few jobs that pay people to work with their hands in such a diverse way.

The down side is that bench jewelers work alone, and our social skills tend to be underdeveloped. Our employers tend to think of us as little jewelry machines that can crank out repair work without showing their appreciation by providing regular breaks and offering their thanks. Our busiest time of the year is the Christmas season when most people would prefer to spend extra time with their families.

Q. What advice would you give to young people who are interested in becoming jewelers?

A. Most of the entry-level jobs are with chain stores, where you won't be encouraged to develop your skills. These positions will burn out young jewelers. You must aggressively develop your skills in the beginning years and at the same time try to move away from low-end, mall-type stores to independents and then to high-end "guild" operations, such as Tiffany's or Cartier. You see, when a bench jeweler first learns to fix jewelry they start doing basic sizings or other minor repair work. As the jeweler's ability develops, then more advanced stone-setting projects are added. After years of experience, a bench jeweler may take on custom fabrication or advanced stone-setting work. Along the way it will serve the jeweler well to have his or her skills tested and obtain one of the four levels of certification through our governing body, Jewelers of America. This journey up the ability ladder can take 10 years to become a certified master bench jeweler, but the climb is worth it. Think of it as a ladder to success, only on this ladder 95 percent of all bench jewelers stay at the bottom, never attempting to move up. If you can get a few steps up, then the path opens dramatically and you can rise up more quickly. The view from the top of the ladder is spectacular, and income warrants the difficulties encountered along the way.

Q. What is the employment outlook for bench jewelers?

A. The profession of bench jeweler, one who repairs and creates jewelry, has for the past four decades been on the decline. Bench jewelers thrived during the early part of the 20th century when independently owned, single jewelry store operations were the norm. Then during the '70s, '80s and '90s chain store operations and mall jewelers began to crowd out the stand-alone jewelry store. In mall jewelry stores, less emphasis is placed on having an in-store bench jeweler. Repair work is often bundled and sent to a central repair facility where it is churned out in near sweat-shop environments. This scenario has degraded the bench jeweler profession to the point that fewer people were seeking these jobs.

That said there are still many exceptions to this rule. Single store and small chain operators now seem to be growing in popularity. This may be due to a higher quality of service these stores can offer. The future for the bench jeweler may today be brighter than it was in the recent past. Unfortunately, the number of people seeking careers as bench jewelers is still on the decline. I've heard stories of store owners finding it more and more difficult to hire a qualified bench jeweler. I believe at some point the rate of pay offered to intro-level bench jewelers will rise and possibly make it a better profession to enter.

Merchandise Displayers

OVERVIEW

Merchandise displayers, sometimes known as *visual merchandisers*, design and install displays of clothing, accessories, furniture, and other products to attract customers. They set up these displays in windows and showcases and on the sales floors of retail stores. Display workers who specialize in dressing mannequins are known as *model dressers*. Those who specialize in installing displays in store windows are known as *window dressers* or *window trimmers*. These workers use their artistic flair and imagination to create excitement and customer interest in the store. They also work with other types of merchandising to develop exciting images, product campaigns, and shopping concepts. There are approximately 86,000 merchandise displayers and window trimmers employed in the United States.

HISTORY

Eye-catching displays of merchandise attract customers and encourage them to buy. This form of advertising has been used throughout history. Farmers who displayed their produce at markets were careful to place their largest, most tempting fruits and vegetables at the top of the baskets. Peddlers opened their bags and cases and arranged their wares in attractive patterns. Store owners decorated their windows with collections of articles they hoped to sell. Their business success

QUICK FACTS

School Subjects
Art
Technical/shop
Theater/dance

Personal Skills
Artistic
Mechanical/manipulative

Work Environment
Primarily indoors
Primarily one location

Minimum Education Level
High school diploma

Salary Range
$15,000 to $22,590 to $39,180+

Certification or Licensing
None available

Outlook
About as fast as the average

DOT
298

GOE
01.02.03

NOC
N/A

O*NET-SOC
27-1026.00

often was a matter of chance, however, and depended heavily on their own persuasiveness and sales ability.

As glass windows became less expensive, storefronts were able to accommodate larger window frames. This exposed more of the store to passersby, and stores soon found that decorative window displays were effective in attracting customers. Today, a customer may see nearly the entire store and the displays of the products it sells just by looking in the front window.

The advent of self-service stores has minimized the importance of the salesperson's personal touch. The merchandise now has to sell itself. Displays have become an important inducement for customers to buy. Advertising will bring people into stores, but an appealing product display can make the difference between a customer who merely browses and one who buys.

Merchandise displayers are needed year-round, but during the Christmas season they often execute their most elaborate work. Small retail stores generally depend on the owner or manager to create the merchandise displays, or they may hire a freelance window dresser on a part-time basis. Large retail operations such as department stores retain a permanent staff of display and visual merchandising specialists. Competition among these stores is intense, and their success depends on capturing a significant portion of the market. Therefore, they allocate a large share of their publicity budget to creating unique, captivating displays.

THE JOB

Using their imagination and creative ability, as well as their knowledge of color harmony, composition, and other fundamentals of art and interior design, merchandise displayers in retail establishments create an idea for a setting designed to show off merchandise and attract customers' attention. Often, the display is planned around a theme or concept. After the display manager approves the design or idea, the display workers create the display. They install background settings such as carpeting, wallpaper, and lighting; gather props and other accessories; arrange mannequins and merchandise; and place price tags and descriptive signs where they are needed.

Displayers may be assisted in some of these tasks by carpenters, painters, or store maintenance workers. Displayers may use merchandise from various departments of the store or props from previous displays. Sometimes they borrow special items that their business doesn't carry from other stores (for example, toys or sports equipment). The displays are dismantled and new ones installed every few weeks. In very large stores that employ many display workers, displayers may specialize in carpentry, painting, making signs, or setting up interior or window displays. A *display director* usually supervises and coordinates the display workers' activities and confers with other managers to select merchandise to be featured.

Ambitious and talented display workers have many possible career avenues. The importance of visual merchandising is being recognized more and more as retail establishments compete for consumer dollars. Some display workers can advance to display director or even to a position in store planning.

In addition to traditional stores, the skills of *visual marketing workers* are now in demand in many other types of establishments. Restaurants often try to present a distinct image to enhance the dining experience. Outlet stores, discount malls, and entertainment centers also use visual marketing to establish their identities with the public. Chain stores often need to make changes in or redesign all their stores and turn to display professionals for their expertise. Consumer product manufacturers also are heavily involved in visual marketing. They hire display and design workers to come up with exciting concepts, such as in-store shops, that present a unified image of the manufacturer's products and are sold as complete units to retail stores.

There are also opportunities for employment with store fixture manufacturers. Many companies build and sell specialized props, banners, signs, displays, and mannequins and hire display workers as sales representatives to promote their products. The display workers' understanding of retail needs and their insight into the visual merchandising industry make them valuable consultants.

This occupation appeals to imaginative, artistic individuals who find it rewarding to use their creative abilities to visualize a design concept and transform it into reality. Original, creative displays grow out of an awareness of current design trends and popular themes. Although display workers use inanimate objects such as props and materials, an understanding of human motivation helps them create displays with strong customer appeal.

REQUIREMENTS

High School

To work as a display worker, you must have at least a high school diploma. Important high school subjects include art, woodworking, mechanical drawing, and merchandising.

Postsecondary Training

Some employers require college courses in art, interior decorating, fashion design, advertising, or related subjects. Community and junior colleges that offer advertising and marketing courses may include display work in the curriculum. Fashion merchandising schools and fine arts institutes also offer courses useful to display workers.

Much of the training for display workers is gained on the job. They generally start as helpers for routine tasks such as carrying props and dismantling sets. Gradually they are permitted to build simple props and work up to constructing more difficult displays. As they become more experienced, display workers who show artistic talent may be assigned to plan simple designs. The total training time varies depending on the beginner's ability and the variety and complexity of the displays.

Other Requirements

Besides education and experience, you will need creative ability, manual dexterity, and mechanical aptitude to do this work. You should possess the strength and physical ability needed to be able to carry equipment and climb ladders. You also need agility to work in close quarters without upsetting props.

EXPLORING

To explore the work of merchandise displayers, try to get a part-time or summer job with a department or retail store or at a convention center. This will give you an overview of the display operations in these establishments. Photographers and theater groups need helpers to work with props and sets, although some may require experience or knowledge related to their work. You school's drama and photo clubs may offer opportunities to learn basic design concepts. You also should read about this line of work; *Display & Design Ideas* (http://www.ddimagazine.com) publishes articles on the field and related subjects.

EMPLOYERS

Approximately 86,000 merchandise displayers and window trimmers are employed in the United States. Most work in department and clothing stores, but many are employed in other types of retail settings such as variety, drug, and shoe stores. Some have their own design businesses, and some are employed by design firms that handle interior and professional window dressing for small stores. Employment of display workers is distributed throughout the country, with most of the jobs concentrated in large towns and cities.

STARTING OUT

School career services offices may have job listings for display workers or related positions. Individuals wishing to become display workers can apply directly to retail stores, decorating firms, or exhibition centers. Openings also may be listed in the classified ads of newspapers.

A number of experienced merchandise displayers choose to work as freelance designers. Competition in this area, however, is intense, and it takes time to establish a reputation, build a list of clients, and earn an adequate income. Freelancing part time while holding down another job provides a more secure income for many display workers. Freelancing also provides beginners with opportunities to develop a portfolio of photographs of their best designs, which they can then use to sell their services to other stores.

ADVANCEMENT

Display workers with supervisory ability can become regional managers. Further advancement may lead to a position as a display director or head of store planning.

Another way to advance is by starting a freelance design business. This can be done with very little financial investment, although freelance design workers must spend many long hours generating new business and establishing a reputation in the field.

Experienced display workers also may be able to transfer their skills to jobs in art-related fields such as interior design or photography. This move, however, requires additional training.

EARNINGS

According to the U.S. Department of Labor, the median annual earnings of merchandise displayers were $22,590 in 2005. The lowest 10 percent earned less than $15,000 and the highest 10 percent earned more than $39,180. Displayers working in clothing stores earned a mean salary of $31,390 in 2005.

Freelance displayers may earn more than $35,000 a year, but their income depends entirely on their talent, reputation, number of clients, and amount of time they work.

Mean Annual Earnings by Industry, 2005

Employer	Mean Annual Earnings
Management of companies and enterprises	$38,220
Apparel and piece goods merchant wholesalers	$34,010
Clothing stores	$31,390
Grocery and related product wholesalers	$27,320
Advertising and related services	$26,590
Alcoholic beverage merchant wholesalers	$25,950
Miscellaneous nondurable goods merchant wholesalers	$22,060

Source: U.S. Department of Labor

WORK ENVIRONMENT

Display workers usually work 35 to 40 hours a week, except during busy seasons such as Christmas. Selling promotions and increased sales drives during targeted seasons can require the display staff to work extra hours in the evening and on weekends.

The work of constructing and installing displays requires prolonged standing, bending, stooping, and working in awkward positions. There is some risk of falling off ladders or being injured from handling sharp materials or tools, but serious injuries are uncommon.

OUTLOOK

Employment for display workers is expected to grow about as fast as the average for all occupations through 2014, according to the U.S. Department of Labor. Growth in this profession is expected due to an expanding retail sector and the increasing popularity of visual merchandising. Most openings will occur as experienced workers retire or leave the occupation.

Fluctuations in our nation's economy affect the volume of retail sales because people are less likely to spend money during recessionary times. For display workers, this can result in layoffs or hiring freezes.

FOR MORE INFORMATION

For information on student membership, scholarship opportunities, schools with student chapters, and additional career materials, contact

American Society of Interior Designers
608 Massachusetts Avenue NE
Washington, DC 20002-6006
Tel: 202-546-3480
http://www.asid.org

For membership information, contact

Institute of Store Planners
25 North Broadway
Tarrytown, NY 10590-
Tel: 914-332-0040
Email: info@ispo.org
http://www.ispo.org

To read about industry events and news, check out the following magazine's Web site

Display & Design Ideas
http://www.ddimagazine.com

Personal Shoppers

OVERVIEW

People who don't have the time or the ability to go shopping for clothes, gifts, groceries, and other items use the services of *personal shoppers*. Personal shoppers shop department stores, look at catalogs, and surf the Internet for the best buys and most appropriate items for their clients. Relying on a sense of style and an ability to spot a bargain, a personal shopper helps clients develop a wardrobe and find gifts for friends, relatives, and employees. Though personal shoppers work all across the country, their services are in most demand in large, metropolitan areas.

HISTORY

For decades, American retailers have been working to create easier ways to shop. Mail-order was an early innovation: Catalog companies such as Montgomery Wards and Sears, Roebuck and Co. started business in the late 19th century to meet the shopping needs of people living in rural areas and small towns. Many consumers relied on mail-order for everything from suits and dresses to furniture and stoves; Sears even sold automobiles through the mail. Shopping for food, clothes, and gifts was considered a household chore, a responsibility that belonged to women. By the late 1800s, shopping had developed into a popular pastime in metropolitan areas. Wealthy women of leisure turned downtown shopping districts into the busiest sections of their cities, as department stores, boutiques, tea shops, and cafés evolved to serve them.

As more women joined the workforce after World War II, retailers worked to make their shopping areas more convenient. Supermarkets, shopping centers, and malls became popular. Toward the end of the 20th century, shoppers began looking for even more simplicity and convenience. In the 1990s, many companies began to market their products via the Internet. In addition to Internet commerce, over-worked men and women are turning to personal shoppers, professional organizers, and personal assistants to fulfill their shopping needs.

THE JOB

Looking for a job where you get to shop all the time, tell people what to wear, and spend somebody else's money? Though this may seem to describe the life of the personal shopper, it's not quite accurate. For one thing, personal shoppers don't get to shop all the time; they will be spending some time in stores and browsing catalogs, but they're often looking for something very specific and working as quickly as they can. And they do not so much tell people what to wear as teach them how to best match outfits, what colors suit them, and what styles are most appropriate for their workplaces. Yes, personal shoppers spend someone else's money, but it's all for someone else's closet. So, if you're not too disillusioned, read on; working as a personal shopper may still be right for you.

Personal shoppers help people who are unable or uninterested in doing their own shopping. They are hired to look for that perfect gift for a difficult-to-please aunt. They work for senior citizens or people with disabilities to do their grocery shopping and run other shopping errands. Personal shoppers help professionals create a nice, complete wardrobe. All the while, they rely on their knowledge of the local marketplace in order to do the shopping quickly and efficiently.

Some personal shoppers use their backgrounds in other areas to assist clients. Those with a background in cosmetology may work as *image consultants*, advising clients on their hair, clothes, and makeup. Another shopper may have some experience in dealing antiques and will help clients locate particular items. An interior decorator may shop for furniture and art to decorate a home.

Personal shoppers who offer wardrobe consultation will need to visit their client's home and evaluate his or her clothes. They help their clients determine what additional clothes and accessories they'll need, and they offer advice on what jackets to wear with what pants or what skirt to wear with what blouse. Together with their client, personal shoppers determine what additional clothes are needed to complete the wardrobe, and they come up with a budget. Then it's off to the stores.

Irene Kato owns I Kan Do It Personal Shopper, Etc., a personal shopping service. She offers a variety of services, including at-home wardrobe consultation, closet organization, and gift-shopping. "Most of my shopping so far has been for clothes," Kato says. "I have a fairly good idea of what I'm looking for so I don't spend too much time in any one store if I don't see what I want right away. I can usually find two or three choices for my client and rarely have to shop another day." Kato spends about two to three hours every other day shopping and about two hours a day in her office working on publicity, her budget, and corresponding with clients. Shopping for one client can take about three hours. "I have always enjoyed shopping," Kato says, "and especially like finding bargains. Waiting in lines, crowds, etc., does not bother me."

Personal shoppers often cater to professionals needing business attire and wardrobe consultation. A smaller part of their business will be shopping for gifts. They may even supplement their business by running other errands, such as purchasing theater tickets, making deliveries, and going to the post office. Many personal shoppers also work as *professional organizers:* They go into homes and offices to organize desks, kitchens, and closets.

In addition to the actual shopping, personal shoppers have administrative responsibilities. They must keep business records, make phone calls, and schedule appointments. Since personal shopping is a fairly new endeavor, personal shoppers must be expert at educating the public about their services. "A personal shopper has no commodity to sell," Kato says, "only themselves. So it is twice as hard to attract clients." To publicize her business, Kato maintains a Web site (http://www.ikandoit.net) that lists the services she provides and testimonials from clients. She also belongs to two professional organizations that help her network and develop her business: Executive Women International and Giving Referrals to Other Women.

REQUIREMENTS

High School

Take classes in home economics to develop budget and consumer skills as well as learn about fashion and home design. If the class offers a sewing unit, you'll learn about tailoring, and you can develop an eye for clothing sizes. Math, business, and accounting courses will prepare you for the administrative details of the job. English composition and speech classes will help you develop the communication skills you'll need to promote your business and advise clients about their wardrobes.

Postsecondary Training

Many people working as personal shoppers have had experience in other areas of business. They've worked as managers in corporations or have worked as salespeople in retail stores. But because of the entrepreneurial nature of the career, you don't need any specific kind of education or training. A small-business course at your local community college, along with classes in design, fashion, and consumer science, can help you develop the skills you'll need for the job. If you're unfamiliar with computers, you should take some classes to learn desktop publishing programs for creating business cards and other publicity material.

Other Requirements

"I seem to have an empathy for people," Irene Kato says. "After talking with a client, I know what they want and what they're looking for. I am a very good listener." In addition to these people skills, a personal shopper should be patient and capable of dealing with the long lines and customer service of department stores. You should be creative and able to come up with a variety of gift ideas. A sense of style is important, along with knowledge of the latest brands and designers. You'll need a good eye for colors and fabrics. You should also be well dressed and organized so that your client will know to trust your wardrobe suggestions.

EXPLORING

If you've spent any time at the mall, you probably already have enough shopping experience. And if you've had to buy clothes and gifts with limited funds, you know something about budgeting. Sign up for the services of a personal shopper in a department store; in most stores, the service is free, and you'll get a sense of how a shopper works. Pay close attention to the information they request from you in the beginning, and ask them later about their decision-making process. Irene Kato advises future personal shoppers to work a few years at a retail clothing store. "This way," she says, "you can observe the way people dress, what shapes and sizes we all are, how fashion trends come and go, and what stays."

EMPLOYERS

Professional men and women with high incomes and busy schedules are the primary employers of personal shoppers. Shoppers may also work with people with new jobs requiring dress clothes but also with

Learn More About It

Entrepreneur Press. *Start Your Own Personal Concierge Service.* Irvine, Calif.: Entrepreneur Press, 2003.

Lumpkin, Emily S. *Get Paid to Shop: Be a Personal Shopper for Corporate America.* Columbia, S.C.: Forte Publishing, 1999.

McBride, Laura Harrison, Peter J. Gallanis, and Tag Goulet. *FabJob Guide to Become a Personal Shopper.* Seattle, Wash.: FabJob.com Ltd., 2005.

Sparklesoup LLC. *Career KNOWtes Personal Shopping (How to Have Fun and Make Money).* Irving, Tex.: Sparklesoup LLC, 2005.

people who need to perk up an old wardrobe. Personal shoppers may work for executives in corporations who need to buy gifts for large staffs of employees. Some of their clients may be elderly or have disabilities and have problems getting out to do their shopping.

STARTING OUT

Start-up costs for personal shoppers can be very low; you may only have to invest in a computer, business cards, and a reliable form of transportation. But it could take you a very long time to develop a regular clientele. You'll want to develop the business part time while still working full time at a more reliable job. Some of your first clients may come from your workplace. Offer free introductory services to a few people and encourage them to spread the word and hand out your business card. You'll also need to become very familiar with the local retail establishments and the discount stores with low-cost, high-quality merchandise.

"My friends and colleagues at work," Irene Kato says, "were always complimentary on what I wore and would ask where I bought my clothes, where they could find certain items, where were the best sales." Kato was taking the part-time approach to developing her personal shopping service, when downsizing at her company thrust her into the new business earlier than she'd planned. She had the opportunity to take an entrepreneurism class at a local private university, which helped her devise a business plan and taught her about the pros and cons of starting a business.

ADVANCEMENT

It takes years of dedication, high-quality work, and referrals to create a successful business. Personal shoppers should expect lean early years as they work to build their business and expand their clientele. After a few years of working part time and providing superior service, a personal shopper may develop his or her business into a full-time endeavor. Eventually, he or she may be able to hire an assistant to help with the administrative work such as client billing and scheduling.

EARNINGS

Personal shoppers bill their clients in different ways: They set a regular fee for services, charge a percentage of the sale, or charge an hourly rate. They might use all these methods in their business; their billing method may depend on the client and the service. For example, when offering wardrobe consultation and shopping for clothes, a personal shopper may find it best to charge by the hour; when shopping for a small gift, it may be more reasonable to charge only a percentage. Personal shoppers charge anywhere from $25 to $125 an hour; the average hourly rate is about $75. Successful shoppers living in a large city can make between $1,500 and $3,000 a month.

WORK ENVIRONMENT

Personal shoppers have all the advantages of owning their own business, including setting their own hours and keeping a flexible schedule. But they also have all the disadvantages, such as job insecurity and lack of benefits. "I have a bad habit of thinking about my business almost constantly," Irene Kato says. Though personal shoppers don't have to deal with the stress of a full-time office job, they will have the stress of finding new clients and keeping the business afloat entirely by themselves.

Although personal shoppers usually work from a home office, they still spend a lot of time with people, from clients to salespeople. They will obviously spend some time in department stores; if they like to shop, this can be enjoyable even when they're not buying anything for themselves. In some cases, personal shoppers visit clients' homes to advise them on their wardrobe. They do a lot of traveling, driving to a department store after a meeting with a client, then back to the client's with the goods.

OUTLOOK

Personal shopping is a new business development, so anyone embarking on the career will be taking some serious risks. There's not a lot of research available about the career, no national professional organization specifically serving personal shoppers, and no real sense of the career's future. The success of Internet commerce will probably have a big effect on the future of personal shopping. If purchasing items through the Internet becomes more commonplace, personal shoppers may have to establish places for themselves on the Web. Some personal shoppers currently with Web sites offer consultation via e-mail and help people purchase products online.

To attract the widest variety of clients, personal shoppers should offer as expansive a service as they can. Professional organizing is being recognized as one of the top home businesses for the future; membership of the National Association of Professional Organizers is growing each year. *Personal assistants*, those who run errands for others, have also caught the attention of industry experts, and programs are available to assist people interested in entering this field.

FOR MORE INFORMATION

For more information on professional networking opportunities for women, contact
Executive Women International
515 South 700 East, Suite 2A
Salt Lake City, UT 84102-2855
Tel: 801-355-2800
Email: ewi@executivewomen.org
http://www.executivewomen.org

To learn about a career as a professional organizer, contact
National Association of Professional Organizers
4700 West Lake Avenue
Glenview, IL 60025-1468
Tel: 847-375-4746
Email: hq@napo.net
http://www.napo.net

Pet Shop Workers

OVERVIEW

Pet shop workers, from entry-level clerks to store managers, are involved in the daily upkeep of a pet store; they sell pets and pet supplies, including food, medicine, toys, carriers, and educational books and videos. They work with customers, answering questions and offering animal care advice. They keep the store, aquariums, and animal cages clean and look after the health of the pets for sale. They also stock shelves, order products from distributors, and maintain records on the animals and products.

HISTORY

Can you imagine George Washington with a pet hamster? No? Well, there's a good reason for that—the hamster wasn't even domesticated until around 1930. But picturing George alongside his faithful steed isn't a problem at all. Just as successful horse trading was important to the development of Indian villages for thousands of years, horse trading proved a staple of American business from the first colonies to the cities of the early 20th century. Though the horses in the stables of the early Americans were well-loved by their owners, they weren't exactly considered "pets" or "companion animals." Horses were relied upon for transportation, industry, and farm work. But these horse traders, with their sense of business and knowledge of animal care, are early examples of the pet shop owners who found thriving business on the town squares across the developing country, alongside the apothecaries and general stores.

Though domestic cats in the United States only date from around 1750, they were first domesticated (along with lions and hyenas) around 1900 BC in Egypt. In the years before that, cats were considered sacred (perhaps explaining the royal bearing of many of today's pampered house cats!). Dogs as pets predate cats; ancient carvings and paintings depict a range of breeds, and Egyptian tomb paintings feature greyhounds and terriers.

THE JOB

The soft barks of the puppies being groomed in the back of the shop; the trills and whistles of the birds in their cages; the bubbling of the fish tanks—these sights and sounds combine to make a visit to the neighborhood pet store unlike any other shopping experience. But running a pet shop calls upon the same business skills required for the operation of any retail establishment. Pet shop workers are in the business to sell to customers; many pet stores employ cashiers, sales and marketing people, managers, and bookkeepers. Pet shop owners may also hire pet groomers, animal caretakers, and animal trainers. A pet shop must have a staff that loves animals, is knowledgeable about pets and their care, and is good with customers.

The top priorities for pet shop workers are animal care and customer care. Though the size of the pet shop will determine how many duties are assigned each worker, most pet shop workers take part in preparing the store for opening; they make sure the shop is clean, the shelves are in order, the aisles are clear, and the cash register is ready for sales. Cages and fish tanks are cleaned, and the animals are fed and watered. Though some pet shops continue to sell dogs and cats, most buyers for those kinds of animals purchase directly from breeders or select animals from shelters and the Humane Society. Today's pet shops generally specialize in birds, fish, and small animals such as hamsters and mice. Once the animals are taken care of, pet shop workers see to the needs of customers. "At a small pet shop, you begin to think of your customers as your friends," says Max Paterson, a high school student who works for a pet shop in Ohio. "I once tried to count how many questions I answered in a day, and when I got past 250, I stopped." Customers rely on pet shop workers for animal care advice and expect them to be knowledgeable not only of the pets for sale but of the food, medicines, and other supplies as well. "The biggest benefits I've received from the job," Paterson says, "are the relationships with the customers, and the huge dictionary of tropical fish I've developed in my head."

Pet shops may offer a variety of services, including pet grooming, dog training, and animal boarding. They may also offer animal vaccinations. A store manager is often responsible for organizing the various services, interviewing and hiring store employees, dealing with distributors, and maintaining records of sales and animal health.

Kathryn Chambliss manages a small pet shop, The Fish Peddler, in Alabama. "This job is a natural outgrowth of my hobby," she says. "I have been breeding and showing dogs since I was a teenager. My children were always bringing home pets and injured animals for me to take care of, and I have always been very active in promoting responsible pet ownership and animal care issues." Both Chambliss and Paterson emphasize that working in a small pet shop is very different from working in the larger, discount superstores. "We cannot match their prices," Chambliss says, "so we have to be better than they are in terms of service, friendliness, and working with the customer."

REQUIREMENTS

High School

For pet store work, you'll need to develop a good business sense, the ability to work well with customers, and knowledge of animals and their care. In high school, accounting, marketing, and other business-related courses are valuable, as are math courses. You'll need math for both money management and for figuring proper feed and medication amounts for the animals. The sciences are important for anyone working with animals. Knowledge of chemistry will come in handy when preparing medications and chemicals for the aquariums. Biology will introduce you to the biological systems of various kinds of animals. Geography courses can also add to your understanding of animals by introducing you to their natural habitats and origins.

A business club such as Future Business Leaders of America will introduce you to area business owners and help you develop skills in advertising, marketing, and management. Agricultural clubs and 4-H clubs can teach you about animal care and responsibilities.

Postsecondary Training

You can easily get work at a pet store without any college education or special training. As with most retail businesses, pet shops often employ high school students for part-time and summer positions. Store owners usually hire people with a love of animals and some knowledge of their care for entry-level positions such as clerk, cashier, and salesperson. For management positions, a pet shop owner may want someone with some higher education. It is also easier to advance into management positions if you have a college degree.

Though any college degree will be valuable for higher-level pet shop positions, you'll want to take courses in marketing, accounting, merchandising, and other business-related areas. Some pet shops also like to hire people with veterinary tech training. Students pursuing a preveterinary sciences degree often work part time in a pet shop to gain experience with animals and their owners.

Because of the wide availability of retail work, you would be better advised to pursue a paid entry-level position at a store rather than an internship. But belonging to a business organization as a student can offer you valuable insight into marketing and management. DECA, an association of marketing students, is an organization that prepares high school and junior college students for retail careers. There are many local chapters of DECA across the country and annual leadership conferences. Some DECA chapters also offer scholarships to marketing students.

Other Requirements

"It takes a great deal of respect and love for animals," Max Paterson says about working in a pet shop, "a person who can help customers even when there are lots of them, and someone who's not afraid to get their hands dirty every now and again." As with any retail job, you must be prepared to serve people on a daily basis—you should be friendly and outgoing and prepared to answer questions clearly and patiently. Though most of your encounters with these fellow animal-lovers will likely be pleasant, you must be prepared for the occasional dissatisfied customer; dealing with angry customers requires you to remain calm and to settle disputes diplomatically. You must remain informed on new products and animal care; customers will be asking you about the right-size cages for particular birds or how many fish a tank can hold. In answering such questions, your first concern must be for the well being of the animals, not for the biggest profit. Some customers may even be testing you with their questions, making sure the store's staff is reliable. Kathryn Chambliss says, "I like just being around the animals, and people who like animals. I like helping people choose the right pet for their lifestyle. I like designing water gardens, and helping customers select the right mix of plant and fish for a beautiful addition to their home."

Depending on your duties at the pet store, you'll need analytical skills; you'll be analyzing data when ordering new products, choosing vendors, and examining sales figures and invoices. In whatever position you fill at the pet store, it will be important for you to manage your time well to deal with customers while keeping the store orderly and the shelves well stocked.

EXPLORING

With the number of volunteer opportunities at animal shelters, zoos, and other animal care facilities, you can easily gain experience working with animals. You may also want to spend a few days "shadowing" some pet shop managers, following them throughout their workday to get a sense of their duties. Max Paterson, before going to work for the pet shop, spent a lot of his spare time there learning about the animals and the products for sale. "The first step was creating a trusting, customer/owner relationship," he says. "From there, I began asking if he needed some odd jobs done for a few bucks, and in doing these jobs, and just hanging out at the store, I began to pick up on all he was saying to the customers. Soon, I too knew enough to help customers."

EMPLOYERS

Pet store workers work in pet stores—from "mom and pop" establishments to large chains such as PETCO and PetSmart.

STARTING OUT

After spending so much time at his local pet shop and learning so much about the business, Max Paterson was able to step into a job. "I now work regular hours," he says, "and have often been left to watch the store on my own." Experience with animal care can help you get a job in a pet store, but such experience is not always required. A pet shop owner or manager may be prepared to give you on-the-job training. You can check the classified ads in your paper for pet shop jobs, but a better approach is to visit all the pet stores in your area and fill out applications. If you don't hear back from the store right away, follow up on a regular basis so that the manager or store owner gets to know you. That way, when there is a job opening, the manager will have you in mind.

For management positions, you should have some background in entry-level retail positions and some college education. While pursuing that education, you can take part-time work in pet stores or other retail businesses. Though any retail experience is valuable, experience in a small pet store will involve you directly with many of the main concerns of a business; in a pet "megastore," your experience may be limited to a few duties.

ADVANCEMENT

The longer you work in one store, the more responsibilities you're likely to be given. After starting as a cashier or stock person, you may eventually be allowed to open and close the store, place orders, create advertisements, order new products, and deal with distributors. Experience in the many different areas of one particular business can lead to advancement from an entry-level position to a management position, even if you don't have a college education.

As a manager, you may be allowed to expand the store in new directions; with the understanding of a store and its clientele, you can introduce such additions as an animal-training program, sponsorship of adopt-a-pet and animal-assisted therapy programs, and new product lines.

EARNINGS

"This is not a business that will ever make us rich," Kathryn Chambliss points out. "Most of the time, the store generates enough in sales to pay bills, and very little else." Entry-level pet shop workers earn minimum wage, and even those with experience probably won't make much more than that. Though the average store manager makes under $30,000, there does seem to be the possibility of salary increases in the future. In order to attract more experienced store managers, store owners are beginning to reward managers for their varied responsibilities and extra hours. The size of the store also makes a difference; stores with larger volumes pay their managers considerably more than stores with volumes of less than $1 million. The size of the store also determines the number of benefits for a full-time employee. In smaller stores, pet shop workers may not receive any health benefits or vacation pay, while a bigger store may have group health plans for managers.

WORK ENVIRONMENT

A clean, healthy pet shop should make for a very comfortable work environment. But to keep the place clean and healthy, workers in this field handle animals, clean out cages and fish tanks, and prepare medications. They also sweep the floors of the store and dust shelves. A pet shop should also be well ventilated and temperature controlled. During work hours, pet shop workers usually stay indoors and don't venture far from their assigned work stations.

Working in a public place devoted to the care of animals, some pet shop workers find themselves taking on extra responsibilities. "Every day," Kathryn Chambliss says, "I have at least one person bring me an abused or uncared-for animal. I provide foster care for baby animals left at the Humane Society, and I try to raise them, wean them, and find them homes. It is tragic that there is so little responsible pet ownership in this country." Though pet shop workers do their best to educate customers and to prepare them for pet ownership, they must still deal with the fact that many animals in their community are without good homes.

OUTLOOK

The larger pet stores, which can afford to offer special pricing, inexpensive grooming facilities, and free training programs, are taking much of the business away from the smaller, traditional, "mom and pop" pet shops. This trend is likely to continue, but small stores will survive as they promote a more personalized and knowledgeable assistance not available at larger stores. The pet retail industry, in some form, will grow along with the retail industry in general.

The puppies and kittens frolicking in the windows of corner pet shops are becoming a thing of the past as animal activists have made the public increasingly aware of "puppy mills" and other unregulated animal breeders. Groups such as the American Society for the Prevention of Cruelty to Animals fight for better regulation of animal sales practices and animal care in pet shops.

Holistic pet care is also changing the industry—nonchemical remedies, natural foods, and vitamin supplements for animals are gaining more acceptance from store owners, animal breeders, and veterinarians. And, as with every industry, computers have influenced the way stores keep records of business, sales, and animal health. Pet shop managers will be expected to have some computer skills and a basic understanding of bookkeeping software.

FOR MORE INFORMATION

For information about pet care, contact
American Society for the Prevention of Cruelty to Animals
424 East 92nd Street
New York, NY 10128-6804
Tel: 212-876-7700
http://www.aspca.org

For information on careers, visit the NRF's Web site.
National Retail Federation (NRF)
325 7th Street, NW, Suite 1100
Washington, DC 20004-2818
Tel: 800-673-4692
http://www.nrf.com

Visit this Web site for information about all kinds of pets.
PetsForum Group
http://petsforum.com

Retail Business Owners

OVERVIEW

Retail business owners are entrepreneurs who start or buy their own businesses or franchise operations. They are responsible for all aspects of a business operation, from planning and ordering merchandise to overseeing day-to-day operations. Retail business owners sell such items as clothing, household appliances, groceries, jewelry, and furniture.

HISTORY

Retailing is a vital commercial activity, providing customers with an opportunity to purchase goods and services from various types of merchants. The first retail outlets in America were trading posts and general stores. At trading posts, goods obtained from Native Americans were exchanged for items imported from Europe or manufactured in other parts of the country. As villages and towns grew, trading posts developed into general stores and began to sell food, farm necessities, and clothing. Typically run by a single person, these stores sometimes served as the post office and became the social and economic center of their communities.

Since World War II, giant supermarkets, discount houses, chain stores, and shopping malls have grown in popularity. Even so, individually owned businesses still thrive, often giving customers more personal and better informed service. Moreover, despite the large growth in retail outlets and the increased competition that has accompanied it, retailing still provides the same important function it did in the early years of the United States.

THE JOB

Although retail business owners sell a wide variety of products, from apples to automobiles, the basic job responsibilities remain the same. Simply stated, the retail business owner must do everything necessary to ensure the successful operation of a business.

There are five major categories of job responsibilities within a retail establishment: merchandising and buying; store operations; sales promotion and advertising; bookkeeping and accounting; and personnel supervision. Merchandising and buying determine the type and amount of actual goods to be sold. Store operations involve maintaining the building and providing for the movement of goods and personnel within the building. Sales promotion and advertising are the marketing methods used to inform customers and potential customers about the goods and services that are available. In bookkeeping and accounting, records are kept of payroll, taxes, and money spent and received. Personnel involves staffing the store with people who are trained and qualified to handle all the work that needs to be done.

The owner must be aware of all aspects of the business operation so that he or she can make informed decisions. Specific duties of an individual owner depend on the size of the store and the number of employees. In a store with more than 10 employees, many of the operational, promotional, and personnel activities may be supervised by a manager. The owner may plan the overall purpose and function of the store and hire a manager to oversee the day-to-day operations. In a smaller store, the owner may also do much of the operational activities, including sweeping the floor, greeting customers, and balancing the accounting books.

In both large and small operations, an owner must keep up to date on product information, as well as on economic and technological conditions that may have an impact on business. This entails reading catalogs about product availability, checking current inventories and prices, and researching and implementing any technological advances that may make the operation more efficient. For example, an owner may decide to purchase data processing equipment to help with accounting functions, as well as to generate a mailing list to inform customers of special sales.

Because of the risks involved in opening a business and the many economic and managerial demands put on individual owners, a desire to open a retail business should be combined with proper management skills, sufficient economic backing, and a good sense of what the public wants. The large majority of retail businesses fail because of a lack of managerial experience on the part of owners.

Franchise ownership, whereby an individual owner obtains a license to sell an existing company's goods or services, grew phenomenally during the 1980s. Franchise agreements enable the person who wants to open a business to receive expert advice from the sponsoring company about location, hiring and training of employees, arrangement of merchandise, display of goods, and record keeping. Some entrepreneurs, however, do not want to be limited to the product lines and other restrictions that accompany running a franchise store. Franchise operations also may fail, but their likelihood of success is greater than that of a totally independent retail store.

REQUIREMENTS

High School

A high school diploma is important in order to understand the basics of business ownership, though there are no specific educational or experiential requirements for this position. Course work in business administration is helpful, as is previous experience in the retail trade. Hard work, constant analysis and evaluation, and sufficient capital are important elements of a successful business venture.

If you are interested in owning a business, you should take courses in mathematics and business management and in business-related subjects such as accounting, typing, and computer science. In addition, pursue English and other courses that enhance your communications skills. Specific skill areas also should be developed. For example, if you want to open an electronics repair shop, you should learn as much about electronics as possible.

Owners of small retail businesses often manage the store and work behind the counter. In such a case, the owner of a meat market is the butcher as well.

Postsecondary Training

As the business environment gets more and more competitive, many people are opting for an academic degree as a way of getting more training. A bachelor's program emphasizing business communications, marketing, business law, business management, and accounting should be pursued. Some people choose to get a master's in business administration or other related graduate degree. There are also special business schools that offer a one- or two-year program in business management. Some correspondence schools also offer courses on how to plan and run a business.

Certification or Licensing

A business license may be a requirement in some states. Individual states or communities may have zoning codes or other regulations specifying what type of business can be located in a particular area. Check with your state's chamber of commerce or department of revenue for more information on obtaining a license, or visit this Web site: http://www.sba.gov/hotlist/license.html.

Other Requirements

Whatever the experience and training, a retail business owner needs a lot of energy, patience, and fortitude to overcome the slow times and other difficulties involved in running a business. Other important personal characteristics include maturity, creativity, and good business judgment. Retail business owners also should be able to motivate employees and delegate authority.

EXPLORING

Working full or part time as a sales clerk or in some other capacity within a retail business is a good way to learn about the responsibilities of operating a business. Talking with owners of small shops is also helpful, as is reading periodicals that publish articles on self-employment, such as *Entrepreneur* magazine (http://www.entrepreneur.com).

Most communities have a chamber of commerce whose members usually will be glad to share their insights into the career of a retail business owner. The Small Business Administration, an agency of the U.S. government, is another source of information.

EMPLOYERS

Retail is the second-largest industry in the United States, employing more than 23 million Americans and generating more than $4.1 trillion in retail sales annually, according to Plunkett Research, Ltd. Over 95 percent of all U.S. retailers are single-store businesses, but they generate less than 50 percent of all retail store sales, according to About.com: Retail Industry.

STARTING OUT

Few people start their career as an owner. Many start as a manager or in some other position within a retail business. While developing managerial skills or while pursuing a college degree or other relevant training, you should decide what type of business you would like to own. Many people decide to buy an existing business because it already has a proven track record and because banks and other lending institutions often are more likely to loan money to an existing facility. A retail business owner should anticipate having at least 50 percent of the money needed to start or buy a business. Some people find it helpful to have one or more partners in a business venture.

Owning a franchise is another way of starting a business without a large capital investment, as franchise agreements often involve some assistance in planning and start-up costs. Franchise operations, however, are not necessarily less expensive to run than a totally independent business.

ADVANCEMENT

Because an owner is by definition the boss, there are limited opportunities for advancement. Advancement often takes the form of expansion of an existing business, leading to increased earnings and prestige. Expanding a business also can entail added risk, as it involves increasing operational costs. A successful franchise owner may be offered an additional franchise location or an executive position at the corporate headquarters.

A small number of successful independent business owners choose to franchise their business operations in different areas. Some owners become part-time consultants, while others teach a course at a college or university or in an adult education program. This teaching often is done not only for the financial rewards but as a way of helping others investigate the option of retail ownership.

EARNINGS

Earnings vary widely and are greatly influenced by the ability of the individual owner, the type of product or service being sold, and existing economic conditions. Some retail business owners may earn less than $15,000 a year, while the most successful owners earn $100,000 or more.

WORK ENVIRONMENT

Retail business owners generally work in pleasant surroundings. Even so, ownership is a demanding occupation, with owners often working six or seven days a week. Working more than 60 hours a week is not unusual, especially during the Christmas season and other busy times. An owner of a large establishment may be able to leave a manager in charge of many parts of the business, but the owner still must be available to solve any pressing concerns. Owners of small businesses often stay in the store throughout the day, spending much of the time on their feet.

A retail business owner may occasionally travel out of town to attend conferences or to solicit new customers and product information. An owner of a small business, especially, should develop close relationships with steady customers.

OUTLOOK

The retail field is extremely competitive, and many businesses fail each year. The most common reason for failure is poor management. Thus people with some managerial experience or training will likely have the best chance at running a successful business.

Increasing unemployment, the weakening of consumer confidence, increased competition from other retailers and direct-marketers, and the growth of Internet businesses are just some of the issues retail businesses will face in the next decade.

FOR MORE INFORMATION

The following foundation conducts research and analysis of women-owned businesses

Center for Women's Business Research
1411 K Street NW, Suite 1350
Washington, DC 20005-3407
Tel: 202-638-3060
Email: info@womensbusinessresearch.org
http://www.womensbusinessresearch.org

For materials on educational programs in the retail industry, contact

National Retail Federation
325 7th Street NW, Suite 1100
Washington, DC 20004-2818
Tel: 800-673-4692
http://www.nrf.com

For a business starter packet with information about their loan program and services, and basic facts about starting a business, contact

U.S. Small Business Administration
409 Third Street SW
Washington, DC 20416-0001
Tel: 800-827-5722
Email: answerdesk@sba.gov
http://www.sbaonline.sba.gov

INTERVIEW

Vicki Cunningham (along with her husband, Howard) is the owner of Cunningham Fine Jewelry in Tulsa, Oklahoma. She discussed her career with the editors of *Careers in Focus: Retail*.

Q. Please tell us about your business.

A. Cunningham Fine Jewelry began 19 years ago in an upstairs office with no inventory and only catalogs to sell from. We quickly grew to add two showcases and within three years changed locations to a bigger office and more showcases. As word spread and our customers were having a hard time finding us, we moved to a street-level location and business continued to grow. We are now located in a major strip center and enjoy watching our business grow. We started out with only one employee (myself) and today we have a staff of eight including myself and my husband. Our shopping center houses mostly "big box" stores, which have been big draws for me. This is our fourth location in 19 years and by far our best. We have been at this location for eight-and-a-half years. Because of the location and the ability of "walk-in" traffic, our business doubled in the first year here and has seen steady growth ever since.

Q. What are your responsibilities as a business owner?

A. As owner of a small, independent store you get to do everything from cleaning the toilets, to buying, to advertising, to bookkeeping. My primary responsibilities are the buying and major bookkeeping. Howard handles the loose diamond buying and the marketing. Together we do the hiring and coaching of our staff.

Q. What are the most important personal and professional qualities for jewelry store owners?

A. I think it is important to be a people person as you deal with the public all the time. Even though we have enough to keep us busy off the sales floor in an independent environment like ours, there are those customers who are only happy buying from the "owners."

Q. What are some of the pros and cons of your career?

A. The good thing about owning your own business is you get to set the rules and only have to answer to yourself; the downside is sometimes when money is tight you are the last one to get paid. Also, it is harder to "leave" work at work when your partner in business is also your spouse. You end up living your business 24/7.

Q. What advice would you give to young people who are interested in becoming business owners?

A. Being committed to self education is a must in this business. You can never take the attitude that "you know it all" and don't need to learn any more. Also, belonging to the professional organizations affiliated with the jewelry business provide unlimited education, information, and networking opportunities. Whatever business you are in, a small business owner needs the opportunities provided by professional organizations to keep them attuned and abreast of what is going on in their industry, and they also provide the best networking opportunities. Other advice would be to work for someone else in the field you are interested in before branching out on your own. Most small business owners are happy to share the ups and downs with aspiring entrepreneurs. There is a lot to be said for "location-location-location," and I would encourage any aspiring business owner to research this completely.

Retail Managers

OVERVIEW

Retail managers are responsible for the profitable operation of retail trade establishments. They oversee the selling of food, clothing, furniture, sporting goods, novelties, and many other items. Their duties include hiring, training, and supervising other employees; maintaining the physical facilities; managing inventory; monitoring expenditurcs and receipts; and maintaining good public relations. Retail managers hold about 2.2 million jobs in the United States.

HISTORY

In the United States, small, family-owned stores have been around for centuries. The first large chain store began to operate in the late 19th century. One of the aims of early chain stores was to provide staples for the pioneers of the newly settled West. Because chain store corporations were able to buy goods in large quantities and store them in warehouses, they were able to undersell private merchants.

The number of retail stores, especially supermarkets, began to grow rapidly during the 1930s. Stores often were owned and operated by chain corporations, which were able to benefit from bulk buying and more sophisticated storage practices. Cheaper transportation also contributed to the growth of retail stores because goods could be shipped and sold more economically.

Unlike the early family-owned stores, giant retail outlets employed large numbers of people, requiring various levels of management to oversee the business. Retail managers were hired to oversee particular areas within department stores, for example, but higher-level managers also were needed to make more general decisions about a company's goals and policies. Today, retailing is the second-largest industry in the United States, employing more than 23 million people.

THE JOB

Retail managers are responsible for every phase of a store's operation. They often are one of the first employees to arrive in the morning and the last to leave at night. Their duties include hiring, training, and supervising other employees; maintaining the physical facilities; managing inventory; monitoring expenditures and receipts; and maintaining good public relations.

Perhaps the most important responsibility of retail managers is hiring and training qualified employees. Managers then assign duties to employees, monitor their progress, promote employees, and increase salaries when appropriate. When an employee's performance is not satisfactory, a manager must find a way to improve the performance or, if necessary, fire him or her.

Managers should be good at working with all different kinds of people. Differences of opinion and personality clashes among employees are inevitable, however, and the manager must be able to restore good feelings among the staff. Managers often have to deal with upset customers and must attempt to restore goodwill toward the store when customers are dissatisfied.

Retail managers keep accurate and up-to-date records of store inventory. When new merchandise arrives, the manager ensures that items are recorded, priced, and displayed or shelved. They must know when stock is getting low and order new items in a timely manner.

Some managers are responsible for merchandise promotions and advertising. The manager may confer with an advertising agency representative to determine appropriate advertising methods for the store. The manager also may decide what products to put on sale for advertising purposes.

The duties of store managers vary according to the type of merchandise sold, the size of the store, and the number of employees. In small, owner-operated stores, managers often are involved in accounting, data processing, marketing, research, sales, and shipping. In large retail corporations, however, managers may be involved in only one or two activities.

Top 10 World Retailers, 2004 (by revenue)

Name	Country of Origin
1. Wal-Mart	USA
2. Carrefour	France
3. Home Depot	USA
4. Metro AG	Germany
5. Tesco	United Kingdom
6. Kroger	USA
7. Costco	USA
8. Target	USA
9. Koninklijke Ahold	Netherlands
10. Aldi GmbH & Co.	Germany

Source: *STORES*/Deloitte and Touche Tohmatsu, *2006 Global Powers of Retailing*

REQUIREMENTS

High School
You will need at least a high school education in order to become a retail manager. Helpful courses include business, mathematics, marketing, and economics. English and speech classes are also important. These courses will teach you to communicate effectively with all types of people, including employees and customers.

Postsecondary Training
Most retail stores prefer applicants with a college degree, and many hire only college graduates. Liberal arts, social sciences, and business are the most common degrees held by retail managers.

To prepare for a career as a retail store manager, take courses in accounting, business, marketing, English, advertising, and computer science. If you are unable to attend college as a full-time student, consider getting a job in a store to gain experience and attend college part time. All managers, regardless of their education, must have good marketing, analytical, communication, and people skills.

Many large retail stores and national chains have established formal training programs, including classroom instruction, for their new employees. The training period may last a week or as long as one year. Training for a department store manager, for example, may include working as a salesperson in several departments in order to learn about the store's operations.

Other Requirements

To be a successful retail manager, you should have good communication skills, enjoy working with and supervising people, and be willing to put in very long hours. Diplomacy often is necessary when creating schedules for workers and in disciplinary matters. There is a great deal of responsibility in retail management and such positions often are stressful. A calm disposition and ability to handle stress will serve you well.

EXPLORING

If you are interested in becoming a retail manager, you may be able to find part-time, weekend, or summer jobs in a clothing store, supermarket, or other retail trade establishment. You can gain valuable work experience through such jobs and will have the opportunity to observe the retail industry to determine whether you are interested in pursuing a career in it. It also is useful to read periodicals that publish articles on the retail field, such as *Stores Online* (http://www.stores.org), published by the National Retail Federation.

EMPLOYERS

There are about 2.2 million retail managers in the United States, and about 36 percent are self-employed (many are store owners). Nearly every type of retail business requires management, though small businesses may be run by their owners. Wherever retail sales are made, there is an opportunity for a management position, though most people have to begin in a much lower job. The food industry employs more workers than nearly any other, and retail food businesses always need managers, though smaller businesses may not pay very well. In general, the larger the business and the bigger the city, the more a retail manager can earn. Most other retail managers work in grocery and department stores, motor vehicle dealerships, and clothing and accessory stores.

STARTING OUT

Many new college graduates are able to find managerial positions through their schools' career services office. Some of the large retail chains recruit on college campuses.

Not all store managers, however, are college graduates. Many store managers are promoted to their positions from jobs of less responsibility within their organization. Some may be in the retail industry for more than a dozen years before being promoted. Those with more education often receive promotions faster.

Regardless of educational background, people interested in the retail industry should consider working in a retail store at least part time or during the summer. Although there may not be an opening when the application is made, there often is a high turnover of employees in retail management, and vacancies occur frequently.

ADVANCEMENT

Advancement opportunities in retailing vary according to the size of the store, where the store is located, and the type of merchandise sold. Advancement also depends on the individual's work experience and educational background.

A store manager who works for a large retail chain, for example, may be given responsibility for a number of stores in a given area or region or transferred to a larger store in another city. Willingness to relocate to a new city may increase an employee's promotional opportunities.

Some managers decide to open their own stores after they have acquired enough experience in the retail industry. After working as a retail manager for a large chain of clothing stores, for example, a person may decide to open a small boutique.

Sometimes, becoming a retail manager involves a series of promotions. A person who works in a supermarket, for example, may advance from clerk, checker, or bagger to a regular assignment in one of several departments in the store. After a period of time, he or she may become an assistant manager and eventually a manager.

EARNINGS

Salaries depend on the size of the store, the responsibilities of the job, and the number of customers served. According to the U.S. Department of Labor, median annual earnings of supervisors of retail sales workers, including commission, were $32,840 in 2005.

Salaries ranged from less than $20,500 to more than $57,420 per year. Mean annual earnings of grocery store managers were $34,700 in 2005, and managers of clothing stores earned $35,160. Those who managed other general merchandise stores earned $29,770, and those who managed home building supply stores ranked among the highest paid at $39,510. Managers who oversee an entire region for a retail chain can earn more than $100,000.

In addition to a salary, some stores offer their managers special bonuses, or commissions, which are typically connected to the store's performance. Many stores also offer employee discounts on store merchandise.

WORK ENVIRONMENT

Most retail stores are pleasant places to work, and managers often are given comfortable offices. Many, however, work long hours. Managers often work six days a week and as many as 60 hours a week, especially during busy times of the year such as the Christmas season. Because holiday seasons are peak shopping periods, it is extremely rare that managers can take holidays off or schedule vacations around a holiday, even if the store is not open on that day.

Although managers usually can get away from the store during slow times, they must often be present if the store is open at night. It is important that the manager be available to handle the store's daily receipts, which usually are put in a safe or taken to a bank's night depository at the close of the business day.

OUTLOOK

Employment of retail managers is expected to grow more slowly than the average for all occupations through 2014, according to the U.S. Department of Labor. Although retailers have reduced their management staff to cut costs and make operations more efficient, there still are good opportunities in retailing. Internet stores and e-commerce ventures will present many new opportunities for retail managers, for example. However, competition for all jobs will probably continue to increase, and computerized systems for inventory control may reduce the need for some managers. Applicants with the best educational backgrounds and work experience will have the best chances of finding jobs. There will always be a need for retail managers, however, as long as retail stores exist. Retail manager positions are rarely affected by corporate restructuring at retail headquarters; this has a greater impact on home office staff.

FOR MORE INFORMATION

For materials on educational programs in the retail industry, contact
National Retail Federation
325 7th Street NW, Suite 1100
Washington, DC 20004-2818
Tel: 800-673-4692
http://www.nrf.com

For information on jobs in retail, contact
Retail Industry Leaders Association
1700 North Moore Street, Suite 2250
Arlington, VA 22209-1933
Tel: 703-841-2300
http://www.retail-leaders.org

Retail Sales Workers

QUICK FACTS

School Subjects
English
Mathematics
Speech

Personal Skills
Communication/ideas
Helping/teaching

Work Environment
Primarily indoors
Primarily one location

Minimum Education Level
High school diploma

Salary Range
$10,712 to $19,140 to
$37,250+

Certification or Licensing
None available

Outlook
About as fast as the average

DOT
290

GOE
09.04.02

NOC
6421

O*NET-SOC
41-2031.00

OVERVIEW

Retail sales workers assist customers with purchases by identifying their needs, showing or demonstrating merchandise, receiving payment, recording sales, and wrapping their purchases or arranging for their delivery. They are sometimes called *sales clerks, retail clerks,* or *salespeople.* There are approximately 4.3 million retail salespersons employed in the United States.

HISTORY

The Industrial Revolution and its techniques of mass production encouraged the development of specialized retail establishments. The first retail outlets in the United States were trading posts and general stores. At trading posts, goods obtained from Native Americans were exchanged for items imported from Europe or manufactured in the eastern United States. Trading posts had to be located on the fringes of settlements and relocated to follow the westward movement of the frontier. As villages and towns grew, what had been trading posts frequently developed into general stores. General stores sold food staples, farm necessities, and clothing. They often served as the local post office and became the social and economic centers of their communities. They were sometimes known as dry goods stores.

A number of changes occurred in the retail field during the second half of the 19th century. The growth of specialized retail stores (such as hardware, feed, grocery, and drugstores) reflected the growing sophistication of available products and customer tastes. The first grocery chain store, which started in New York City in 1859, led to a new concept in retailing. Later, merchants such as Marshall Field developed huge department stores, so named because of their large number of separate departments. Their variety of merchandise, ability to advertise their products, and low prices contributed to the rapid growth and success of such stores. Retail sales workers staffed the departments, and for the public they became the stores' primary representatives.

The 20th century witnessed the birth of supermarkets and suburban shopping centers, the emergence of discount houses, and the expansion of credit buying. Today, retailing is the second-largest industry in the United States. Grocery stores and food and beverage stores have the highest annual sales in the retail field. Other areas with high annual sales include motor vehicle and parts dealers; department stores; restaurants and cafeterias; lumber and building suppliers; drug and proprietary stores; furniture stores; variety stores; liquor stores; hardware stores; and jewelry stores. All of these retailers hire sales workers.

THE JOB

Salespeople work in more than a hundred different types of retail establishments in a variety of roles. Some, for example, work in small specialty shops where, in addition to waiting on customers, they might check inventory, order stock from sales representatives (or by telephone or mail), place newspaper display advertisements, prepare window displays, and rearrange merchandise for sale.

Other salespeople may work in specific departments, such as the furniture department, of a large department store. The employees in a department work in shifts to provide service to customers six or seven days a week. To improve their sales effectiveness and knowledge of merchandise, they attend regular staff meetings. The work of retail salespeople is supported by advertising, window decorating, sales promotion, buying, and market research specialists.

Whatever they are selling, the primary responsibility of retail sales workers is to interest customers in the merchandise. This might be done by describing the product's features, demonstrating its use, or showing various models and colors. Some retail sales workers must have specialized knowledge, particularly those who sell such expensive, complicated products as stereos, appliances, and personal computers.

In addition to selling, most retail sales workers make out sales checks; receive cash, checks, and charge payments; bag or package purchases; and give change and receipts. Depending on the hours they work, retail sales workers might have to open or close a cash

A retail sales worker shows the extra cushioning in a shoe to a customer. *(Omni Photo Communications Inc./Index Stock Imagery)*

register. This might include counting the money in a cash register; separating charge slips, coupons, and exchange vouchers; and making deposits at the cash office. The sales records they keep are normally used in inventory control. Sales workers are often held responsible for the contents of their registers, and repeated shortages are cause for dismissal in many organizations.

Sales workers must be aware of any promotions the store is sponsoring and know the store's policies and procedures, especially on returns and exchanges. Also, they often must recognize possible security risks and know how to handle such situations.

Consumers often form their impressions of a store by its sales force. To stay ahead in the fiercely competitive retail industry, employers are increasingly stressing the importance of providing courteous and efficient service. When a customer wants an item that is not on the sales floor, for example, the sales worker might be expected to check the stockroom and, if necessary, place a special order or call another store to locate the item.

REQUIREMENTS

High School
Employers generally prefer to hire high school graduates for most sales positions. Such subjects as English, speech, and mathematics

provide a good background for these jobs. Many high schools and two-year colleges have special programs that include courses in merchandising, principles of retailing, and retail selling.

Postsecondary Training
In retail sales, as in other fields, the level of opportunity tends to coincide with the level of a person's education. In many stores, college graduates enter immediately into on-the-job training programs to prepare them for management assignments. Successful and experienced workers who do not have a degree might also qualify for these programs. Useful college courses include economics, business administration, and marketing. Many colleges offer majors in retailing. Executives in many companies express a strong preference for liberal arts graduates, especially those with some business courses or a master's degree in business administration.

Other Requirements
The retail sales worker must be in good health. Many selling positions require standing most of the day. The sales worker must have stamina to face the grueling pace of busy times, such as weekends and the Christmas season, while at the same time remaining pleasant and effective. Personal appearance is important. Salespeople should be neat and well groomed and have an outgoing personality.

A pleasant speaking voice, natural friendliness, tact, and patience are all helpful personal characteristics. The sales worker must be able to converse easily with strangers of all ages. In addition to possessing interpersonal skills, sales workers must be equally good with figures. They should be able to add and subtract accurately and quickly and operate cash registers and other types of business machines.

Most states have established minimum standards that govern retail employment. Some states set a minimum age of 14, require at least a high school diploma, or prohibit more than eight hours of work a day or 48 hours in any six days. These requirements are often relaxed for those people employed during the Christmas season.

EXPLORING
Because of its seasonal nature, retailing offers numerous opportunities for temporary or part-time sales experience. Most stores add personnel for the Christmas season. Vacation areas may hire sales employees, usually high school or college students. Fewer sales positions are available in metropolitan areas during the summer, as this is frequently the slowest time of the year.

Many high schools and junior colleges have developed "distributive education" programs that combine courses in retailing with part-time work in the field. The distributive education student may receive academic credit for this work experience in addition to regular wages. Store owners cooperating in these programs often hire students as full-time personnel upon completion of the program.

EMPLOYERS

About 4.3 million people are employed as sales workers in retail stores of all types and sizes. There are many different types of retail establishments, ranging from small specialty shops that appeal to collectors to large retailers, like Wal-Mart or Target, that sell everything from eyeglasses to DVD players. The largest employers of retail salespersons are department stores; clothing and accessories stores; building material and garden equipment stores; other general merchandise stores; and motor vehicle and parts dealers. Retail sales workers can have just one or two coworkers or well over 100, depending on the size of the establishment.

STARTING OUT

If they have openings, retail stores usually hire beginning salespeople who come in and fill out an application. Major department stores maintain extensive personnel departments, while in smaller stores the manager might do the hiring. Occasionally, sales applicants are given an aptitude test.

Young people might be hired immediately for sales positions. Often, however, they begin by working in the stockroom as clerks, helping to set up merchandise displays, or assisting in the receiving or shipping departments. After a while they might be moved up to a sales assignment.

Training varies with the type and size of the store. In large stores, the beginner might benefit from formal training courses that discuss sales techniques, store policies, the mechanics of recording sales, and an overview of the entire store. Programs of this type are usually followed by on-the-job sales supervision. The beginner in a small store might receive personal instruction from the manager or a senior sales worker, followed by supervised sales experience.

College graduates and people with successful sales experience often enter executive training programs (sometimes referred to as *flying squads* because they move rapidly through different parts of the store). As they rotate through various departments, trainees are exposed to merchandising methods, stock and inventory control, advertising, buying, credit, and personnel. By spending time in each of these areas, trainees receive a broad retailing background designed to help them as they advance into the ranks of management.

ADVANCEMENT

Large stores have the most opportunities for promotion. Retailing, however, is a mobile field, and successful and experienced people can readily change employment. This is one of the few fields where, if the salesperson has the necessary initiative and ability, advancement to executive positions is possible regardless of education.

When first on the job, sales workers develop their career potential by specializing in a particular line of merchandise. They become authorities on a certain product line, such as sporting equipment, women's suits, or building materials. Many good sales workers prefer the role of the senior sales worker and remain at this level. Others might be asked to become supervisor of a section. Eventually they might develop into a department manager, floor manager, division or branch manager, or general manager.

People with sales experience often enter related areas such as buying. Other retail store workers advance into support areas such as personnel, accounting, public relations, and credit.

Young people with ability find that retailing offers the opportunity for unusually rapid advancement. One study revealed that half of all retail executives are under 35 years of age. It is not uncommon for a person under 35 to be in charge of a retail store or department with an annual sales volume of over $1,000,000. Conversely, the retail executive who makes bad merchandising judgments might quickly be out of a job.

EARNINGS

Most beginning sales workers start at the federal minimum wage, which is $5.15 an hour. Wages vary greatly, depending primarily on the type of store and the degree of skill required. Businesses might offer higher wages to attract and retain workers. Some sales workers make as much as $12 an hour or more.

Department stores or retail chains might pay more than smaller stores. Higher wages are paid for positions requiring a greater degree of skill. Many sales workers also receive a commission (often four to eight percent) on their sales or are paid solely on commission. According to the U.S. Department of Labor, median hourly earnings of retail salespersons, including commission, were $9.20 in 2005. Wages ranged from less than $6.54 to more than $17.91 an hour. Sales workers in new and used car dealerships earned mean wages of $20.65 an hour; in building materials, $12.19; in clothing stores, $9.44; and in department stores, $9.31.

Salespeople in many retail stores are allowed a discount on their own purchases, ranging from 10 to 25 percent. This privilege is sometimes extended to the worker's family. Meals in employee cafeterias maintained by large stores might be served at a price below cost. Many stores provide sick leave, medical and life insurance, and retirement benefits for full-time workers. Most stores give paid vacations.

WORK ENVIRONMENT

Retail sales workers generally work in clean, comfortable, well-lighted areas. Those with seniority have reasonably good job security. When business is slow, stores might curtail hiring and not fill vacancies that occur. Most stores, however, are able to weather mild business recessions without having to release experienced sales workers. During periods of economic recession, competition among salespeople for job openings can become intense.

With nearly 2 million retail stores across the country, sales positions are found in every region. An experienced salesperson can find employment in almost any state. The vast majority of positions, however, are located in large cities or suburban areas.

The five-day, 40-hour workweek is the exception rather than the rule in retailing. Most salespeople can expect to work some evening and weekend hours, and longer than normal hours might be scheduled during Christmas and other peak periods. In addition, most retailers restrict the use of vacation time between Thanksgiving and early January. Most sales workers receive overtime pay during Christmas and other rush seasons. Part-time salespeople generally work at peak hours of business, supplementing the full-time staff. Because competition in the retailing business is keen, many retailers work under pressure. The sales worker might not be directly involved but will feel the pressures of the industry in subtle ways. The sales worker must be able to adjust to alternating periods of high activity and monotony. No two days—or even customers—are alike.

Because some customers are hostile and rude, salespeople must learn to exercise tact and patience at all times.

OUTLOOK

The employment of sales personnel should grow about as fast as the average for all occupations through 2014, according to the U.S. Department of Labor. Turnover among sales workers is much higher than average. Many of the expected employment opportunities will stem from the need to replace workers. Other positions will result from existing stores' staffing for longer business hours or reducing the length of the average employee workweek.

As drug, variety, grocery, and other stores have rapidly converted to self-service operations, they will need fewer sales workers. At the same time, many products such as stereo components, electrical appliances, computers, and sporting goods do not lend themselves to self-service operations. These products require extremely skilled sales workers to assist customers and explain the benefits of various makes and models. On balance, as easy-to-sell goods will be increasingly marketed in self-service stores, the demand in the future will be strongest for sales workers who are knowledgeable about particular types of products.

During economic recessions, sales volume and the resulting demand for sales workers generally decline. Purchases of costly items such as cars, appliances, and furniture tend to be postponed during difficult economic times. In areas of high unemployment, sales of all types of goods might decline. Since turnover of sales workers is usually very high, however, employers often can cut payrolls simply by not replacing all those who leave.

There should continue to be good opportunities for temporary and part-time workers, especially during the holidays. Stores are particularly interested in people who, by returning year after year, develop good sales backgrounds.

FOR MORE INFORMATION

For materials on educational programs in the retail industry, contact
National Retail Federation
325 7th Street NW, Suite 1100
Washington, DC 20004-2818
Tel: 800-673-4692
http://www.nrf.com

Sales Representatives

OVERVIEW

Sales representatives, also called *sales reps*, sell the products and services of manufacturers and wholesalers. They look for potential customers or clients such as retail stores, other manufacturers or wholesalers, government agencies, hospitals, and other institutions; explain or demonstrate their products to these clients; and attempt to make a sale. The job may include follow-up calls and visits to ensure the customer is satisfied.

Sales representatives work under a variety of titles. Those employed by manufacturers are typically called *manufacturers' sales workers* or *manufacturers' representatives*. Those who work for wholesalers are sometimes called *wholesale trade sales workers* or *wholesale sales representatives*. A *manufacturers' agent* is a self-employed salesperson who agrees to represent the products of various companies. Approximately 1.9 million people work as manufacturers' and wholesale sales representatives in the United States.

HISTORY

Sales representatives for manufacturers and wholesalers have long played an important role in the U.S. economy. By representing products and seeking out potential customers, they have helped in the efficient distribution of large amounts of merchandise.

The earliest wholesalers were probably the ship "chandlers," or suppliers, of colonial New England, who assembled in large quantities the food and equipment required by merchant ships and military vessels. Ship owners found that a centralized supply source enabled them to equip their vessels quickly.

Various developments in the 19th century made wholesalers more prominent. Factories were becoming larger, thus allowing for huge amounts of merchandise to be manufactured or assembled in a single location. New forms of transportation, especially the railroad, made it more practical for manufacturers to sell their products over great distances. Although some manufacturers would sell their goods directly to retail outlets and elsewhere, many found it easier and more profitable to let wholesalers do this job. Retail stores, moreover, liked working with wholesalers, who were able to sell them a wide range of merchandise from different manufacturers and from different areas of the country and the world.

Sales representatives hired by manufacturers and wholesalers were typically given a specific territory in which to sell their goods. Armed with illustrated product catalogs, special promotional deals, and financial support for advertising, they traveled to prospective customers and tried to explain the important qualities of their products. Competition among sales representatives sometimes was fierce, leading some to be less than scrupulous. Product claims were exaggerated, and retail stores were sometimes supplied with shoddy merchandise. Eventually, more fact-based sales pitches were emphasized by manufacturers and wholesalers, who in the long run benefited from having responsible, honest, well-informed representatives. Products also began to be backed by written guarantees of quality.

Changes in the 20th century, once again including improvements in transportation, brought still more possibilities for sales representatives. Automobiles allowed representatives to travel to many more communities and to carry more product samples and descriptive catalogs. Trucks provided a new means of transporting merchandise. The growth of commercial aviation further expanded the opportunities for salespeople. Sales representatives would eventually be able to travel to customers in New York, Atlanta, Los Angeles, and Minneapolis, for example, all during a single week.

By the late 20th century, the food products industry was one of the largest employers of sales representatives. Other important fields included printing; publishing; fabricated metal products; chemicals and dyes; electrical and other machinery; and transportation equipment. Among the many establishments helped by sales representatives were retail outlets (which needed a constant supply of clothing, housewares, and other consumer goods) and hospitals (which purchased specialized surgical instruments, drugs, rubber gloves, and thousands of other products from representatives).

THE JOB

Manufacturers' representatives and wholesale sales representatives sell goods to retail stores, other manufacturers and wholesalers, government agencies, and various institutions. They usually do so within a specific geographical area. Some representatives concentrate on just a few products. An electrical appliance salesperson, for example, may sell 10 to 30 items ranging from food freezers and air conditioners to waffle irons and portable heaters. Representatives of drug wholesalers, however, may sell as many as 50,000 items.

The duties of sales representatives usually include locating and contacting potential clients, keeping a regular correspondence with existing customers, determining their clients' needs, and informing them of pertinent products and prices. They also travel to meet with clients, show them samples or catalogs, take orders, arrange for delivery, and possibly provide installation. A sales representative also must handle customer complaints, keep up to date on new products, and prepare reports. Many salespeople attend trade conferences, where they learn about products and make sales contacts.

Finding new customers is one of the most important tasks. Sales representatives often follow leads suggested by other clients, from advertisements in trade journals, and from participants in trade shows and conferences. They may make "cold calls" to potential clients. Sales representatives frequently meet with and entertain prospective clients during evenings and weekends.

Other sales workers, called *detail people,* do not engage in direct selling activities but strive instead to create a better general market for their companies' products. A detail person for a drug company, for example, may call on physicians and hospitals to inform them of new products and distribute samples.

The particular products sold by the sales representative directly affect the nature of the work. Salespeople who represent sporting goods manufacturers may spend most of their time driving from town to town calling on retail stores that carry sporting equipment. They may visit with coaches and athletic directors of high schools and colleges. A representative in this line may be a former athlete or coach who knows intimately the concerns of his or her customers.

Food manufacturers and wholesalers employ large numbers of sales representatives. Because these salespeople usually know the grocery stores and major chains that carry their products, their main focus is to ensure the maximum sales volume. Representatives negotiate with retail merchants to obtain the most advantageous store and shelf position for displaying their products. They encourage the store or chain to advertise their products, sometimes by offering to pay part of the advertising costs or by reducing the selling price to the merchant so that a special sale price can be offered to customers. Representatives check to make sure that shelf items are neatly arranged and that the store has sufficient stock of their products.

Sales transactions can involve huge amounts of merchandise, sometimes worth millions of dollars. For example, in a single transaction, a washing-machine manufacturer, construction company, or automobile manufacturer may purchase all the steel products it needs for an extended period of time. Salespeople in this field may do much of their business by telephone because the product they sell is standardized and, to the usual customer, requires no particular description or demonstration.

REQUIREMENTS

High School

A high school diploma is required for most sales positions, although an increasing number of salespeople are graduates of two- or four-year colleges. In high school, take classes such as business, mathematics, psychology, speech, and economics that will teach you to deal with customers and financial transactions.

Postsecondary Training

The more complex a product, the greater the likelihood that it will be sold by a college-trained person. Some areas of sales require specialized college work. Those in engineering sales, for example, usually have a college degree in a relevant engineering field. Other fields that demand specific college degrees include chemical sales (chemistry or chemical engineering), office systems (accounting or business administration), and pharmaceuticals and drugs (biology, chemistry, or pharmacy). Those in less technical sales positions usually benefit from course work in English, speech, psychology, marketing, public relations, economics, advertising, finance, accounting, and business law.

Certification or Licensing

The Manufacturers' Representatives Educational Research Foundation offers several certification designations for sales representatives employed by manufacturers. Contact the foundation for more information.

Other Requirements

To be a successful sales representative, you should enjoy working with people. You should also be self-confident, enthusiastic, and disciplined. You must be able to handle rejection, since only a small number of your contacts will result in a sale.

EXPLORING

If you are interested in becoming a sales representative, try to get part-time or summer work in a retail store. Working as a telemarketer also is useful. Some high schools and junior colleges offer programs that combine classroom study with work experience in sales.

Various opportunities exist that provide experience in direct selling. You can take part in sales drives for school or community groups.

Occasionally, manufacturers hire college students for summer assignments. These temporary positions provide an opportunity for the employer and employee to appraise each other. A high percentage of students hired for these specialized summer programs become

Learn More About It

Colombo, George W. *Start Your Retail Career.* Irvine, Calif.: Entrepreneur Press, 2007.

Dolber, Roslyn. *Opportunities in Retailing Careers.* New York: McGraw-Hill, 2003.

Princeton Review. *Best Entry Level Jobs.* New York: Princeton Review, 2005.

Varley, Rosemary. *Retail Product Management: Buying and Merchandising.* 2nd ed. New York: Routledge, 2005.

WetFeet. *Careers in Retail, 2006 Edition: WetFeet Insider Guide.* San Francisco: WetFeet, Inc., 2005.

Wrice, Mark. *First Steps in a Retail Career.* 2nd ed. New York: Palgrave MacMillan, 2002.

career employees after graduation. Some wholesale warehouses also offer temporary or summer positions.

EMPLOYERS

In the United States, 1.9 million people work as manufacturers' and wholesale sales representatives. About half of these salespeople work in wholesale, many as sellers of machinery. Many others work in mining and manufacturing. Food, drugs, electrical goods, hardware, and clothing are among the most common products sold by sales representatives.

STARTING OUT

Firms looking for sales representatives sometimes list openings with high school and college career services offices, as well as with public and private employment agencies. In many areas, professional sales associations refer people to suitable openings. Contacting companies directly also is recommended. A list of manufacturers and wholesalers can be found in telephone books and industry directories, which are available at public libraries.

Although some high school graduates are hired for manufacturers' or wholesale sales jobs, many join a company in a nonselling position, such as office, stock, or shipping clerk. This experience allows an employee to learn about the company and its products. From there, he or she eventually may be promoted to a sales position.

Most new representatives complete a training period before receiving a sales assignment. In some cases, new salespeople rotate through several departments of an organization to gain a broad exposure to the company's products. Large companies often use formal training programs lasting two years or more, while small organizations frequently rely on supervised sales experience.

ADVANCEMENT

New representatives usually spend their early years improving their sales ability, developing their product knowledge, and finding new clients. As sales workers gain experience, they may be shifted to increasingly larger territories or more difficult types of customers. In some organizations, experienced sales workers narrow their focus. For example, an office equipment sales representative may work solely on government contracts.

Advancement to management positions such as regional or district manager also is possible. Some representatives, however, choose to remain in basic sales. Because of commissions, they often earn more money than their managers do, and many enjoy being in the field and working directly with their customers.

A small number of representatives decide to become *manufacturers' agents,* self-employed salespeople who handle products for various organizations. Agents perform many of the same functions as sales representatives but usually on a more modest scale.

EARNINGS

Many beginning sales representatives are paid a salary while receiving their training. After assuming direct responsibility for a sales territory, they may receive only a commission (a fixed percentage of each dollar sold). Also common is a modified commission plan (a lower rate of commission on sales plus a low base salary). Some companies provide bonuses to successful representatives.

Because manufacturers' and wholesale sales representatives typically work on commission, salaries vary widely. Some made as little as $24,930 a year in 2005, according to the U.S. Department of Labor (USDL). The most successful representatives earned more than $115,340. However, the median annual salaries for sales representatives were $60,760 for those working with technical and scientific products and $47,380 for those working in other aspects of wholesale and manufacturing. Most sales representatives make between $33,000 and $86,000 a year.

Earnings can be affected by changes in the economy or industry cycles, and great fluctuations in salary from year to year or month to month are common. Employees who travel usually are reimbursed for transportation, hotels, meals, and client entertainment expenses.

Sales representatives typically receive vacation days, medical and life insurance, and retirement benefits. However, manufacturers' agents do not receive benefits.

WORK ENVIRONMENT

Salespeople generally work long and irregular hours. Those with large territories may spend all day calling and meeting customers in one city and much of the night traveling to the place where they will make the next day's calls and visits. Sales workers with a small territory may do little overnight travel but, like most sales workers, may spend many evenings preparing reports, writing up orders, and entertaining customers. Several times a year, sales workers may travel to company meetings and participate in trade conventions and conferences. Irregular working hours, travel, and the competitive demands of the job can be disruptive to ordinary family life.

Sales work is physically demanding. Representatives often spend most of the day on their feet. Many carry heavy sample cases or catalogs. Occasionally, sales workers assist a customer in arranging a display of the company's products or moving stock items. Direct sellers must treat customers, even those who are rude or impatient, with tact and courtesy.

OUTLOOK

Employment for manufacturers' and wholesale sales representatives is expected to grow at an average rate through 2014, according to the U.S. Department of Labor. Because of continued economic growth and an increasing number of new products on the market, more sales representatives will be needed to explain, demonstrate, and sell these products to customers. The Department of Labor notes that job opportunities will be better for wholesale sales representatives compared to those of manufacturing sales representatives, as manufacturing firms will rely less on in-house sales personnel. They will instead employ the services of independent sales workers, who are paid exclusively on a commission basis. Although this decreases overhead costs for manufacturers, the instability of self-employment is a deterrent in the field of independent sales. Thus, competition for in-house sales positions with wholesalers will be stiff, and jobs will go to applicants with the most experience and technical knowledge.

Future opportunities will vary greatly depending upon the specific product and industry. For example, as giant food chains replace independent grocers, fewer salespeople will be needed to sell groceries to individual stores. By contrast, greater opportunities will probably exist in the air-conditioning field, and advances in consumer electronics and computer technology also may provide many new opportunities.

FOR MORE INFORMATION

For a list of marketing programs and detailed career information, contact
Direct Marketing Association
Educational Foundation
1120 Avenue of the Americas
New York, NY 10036-6700
Tel: 212-768-7277
http://www.the-dma.org

For referrals to industry trade associations, contact
Manufacturers' Agents National Association
One Spectrum Pointe, Suite 150
Lake Forest, CA 92630-2286
Tel: 877-626-2776
Email: MANA@MANAonline.org
http://www.manaonline.org

For information on certification, contact
Manufacturers' Representatives Educational Research Foundation
8329 Cole Street
Arvada, CO 80005-5834
Tel: 303-463-1801
Email: info@mrerf.org
http://www.mrerf.org

Stock Clerks

OVERVIEW

Stock clerks receive, unpack, store, distribute, and record the inventory for materials or products used by a company, plant, or store. Approximately 1.6 million stock clerks are employed in the United States.

HISTORY

Almost every type of business establishment imaginable—shoe store, auto repair shop, supermarket, hospital, or steel mill—buys materials or products from outside distributors and uses these materials in its operations. A large part of the company's money is tied up in these inventory stocks, but without them operations would come to a standstill. Stores would run out of merchandise to sell, mechanics would be unable to repair cars until new parts were shipped in, and factories would be unable to operate once their basic supply of raw materials ran out.

To avoid these problems, businesses have developed their own inventory-control systems to store enough goods and raw materials for uninterrupted operations, move these materials to the places they are needed, and know when it is time to order more. These systems are the responsibility of stock clerks.

QUICK FACTS

School Subjects
English
Mathematics

Personal Skills
Following instructions

Work Environment
Primarily indoors
Primarily one location

Minimum Education Level
High school diploma

Salary Range
$10,712 to $20,100 to $33,760+

Certification or Licensing
None available

Outlook
Decline

DOT
222

GOE
05.09.01

NOC
1474

O*NET-SOC
43-5081.00, 43-5081.01, 43-5081.02, 43-5081.03, 43-5081.04

THE JOB

Stock clerks work in just about every type of industry, and no matter what kind of storage or stock room they staff—food, clothing, merchandise, medicine, or raw materials—the work of stock clerks is essentially the same. They receive, sort, put away, distribute, and

157

keep track of the items a business sells or uses. Their titles sometimes vary based on their responsibilities.

When goods are received in a stockroom, stock clerks unpack the shipment and check the contents against documents such as the invoice, purchase order, and bill of lading, which lists the contents of the shipment. The shipment is inspected, and any damaged goods are set aside. Stock clerks may reject or send back damaged items or call vendors to complain about the condition of the shipment. In large companies, *shipping and receiving clerks* may do this work.

Once the goods are received, stock clerks organize them and sometimes mark them with identifying codes or prices so they can be placed in stock according to the existing inventory system. In this way the materials or goods can be found readily when needed, and inventory control is much easier. In many firms, stock clerks use handheld scanners and computers to keep inventory records up to date.

In retail stores and supermarkets, stock clerks may bring merchandise to the sales floor and stock shelves and racks. In stockrooms and warehouses, they store materials in bins, on the floor, or on shelves. In settings such as restaurants, hotels, and factories, stock clerks deliver goods when they are needed. They may do this on a regular schedule or at the request of other employees or supervisors. Although many stock clerks use mechanical equipment, such as forklifts, to move heavy items, some perform strenuous and laborious work. In general, the work of a stock clerk involves much standing, bending, walking, stretching, lifting, and carrying.

When items are removed from the inventory, stock clerks adjust records to reflect the products' use. These records are kept as current as possible, and inventories are periodically checked against these records. Every item is counted, and the totals are compared with the records on hand or the records from the sales, shipping, production, or purchasing departments. This helps identify how fast items are being used, when items must be ordered from outside suppliers, or even whether items are disappearing from the stockroom. Many retail establishments use computerized cash registers that maintain an inventory count automatically as they record the sale of each item.

The duties of stock clerks vary depending on their place of employment. Stock clerks working in small firms perform many different tasks, including shipping and receiving, inventory control, and purchasing. In large firms, responsibilities may be more narrowly defined. More specific job categories include *inventory clerks, stock control clerks, material clerks, order fillers, merchandise distributors,* and *shipping and receiving clerks.*

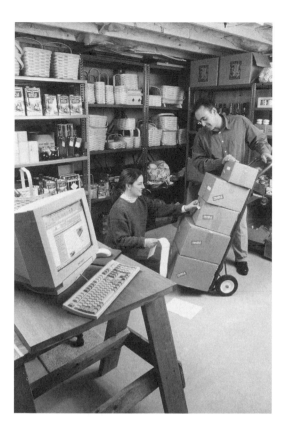

Stock clerks prepare for an order for shipment. (Index Stock Imagery)

REQUIREMENTS

High School

Although there are no specific educational requirements for beginning stock clerks, employers prefer to hire high school graduates. Reading and writing skills and a basic knowledge of mathematics are necessary; typing and filing skills are also useful. In the future, as more companies install computerized inventory systems, knowledge of computer operations will be important.

Other Requirements

Good health and good eyesight is important. A willingness to take orders from supervisors and others is necessary for this work, as is the ability to follow directions. Organizational skills also are important, as is neatness. Depending on where you work, you may be required to join a union. This is especially true of stock clerks who are employed by industry and who work in large cities with a high percentage of union-affiliated companies.

When a stock clerk handles certain types of materials, extra training or certification may be required. Generally, those who handle jewelry, liquor, or drugs must be bonded.

EXPLORING

The best way to learn about the responsibilities of a stock clerk is to get a part-time or summer job as a sales clerk, stockroom helper, stockroom clerk, or, in some factories, stock chaser. These jobs are relatively easy to get and can help you learn about stock work, as well as about the duties of workers in related positions. This sort of part-time work can also lead to a full-time job.

EMPLOYERS

About 1.6 million people work as stock clerks. More than 75 percent of stock clerks work in retail and wholesale firms, and the remainder work in hospitals, factories, government agencies, schools, and other organizations. Nearly all sales-floor stock clerks are employed in retail establishments, especially supermarkets and department stores.

STARTING OUT

Job openings for stock clerks often are listed in newspaper classified ads. Job seekers should contact the personnel office of the firm looking for stock clerks and fill out an application for employment. School counselors, parents, relatives, and friends also can be good sources for job leads and may be able to give personal references if an employer requires them.

Stock clerks usually receive on-the-job training. New workers start with simple tasks such as counting and marking stock. The basic responsibilities of the job are usually learned within the first few weeks. As they progress, stock clerks learn to keep records of incoming and outgoing materials, take inventories, and place orders. As wholesale and warehousing establishments convert to automated inventory systems, stock clerks need to be trained to use the new equipment. Stock clerks who bring merchandise to the sales floor and stock shelves and sales racks need little training.

ADVANCEMENT

Stock clerks with ability and determination have a good chance of being promoted to jobs with greater responsibility. In small firms, stock clerks may advance to sales positions or become assistant buyers or purchasing agents. In large firms, stock clerks can advance to more responsible stock-handling jobs, such as invoice clerk, stock control clerk, and procurement clerk.

Furthering one's education can lead to more opportunities for advancement. By studying at a technical or business school or taking home-study courses, stock clerks can prove to their employer that they have the intelligence and ambition to take on more important tasks. Advanced positions such as warehouse manager and purchasing agent are usually given to experienced people who have post-high school education.

EARNINGS

Beginning stock clerks usually earn the minimum wage or slightly more. The U.S. Department of Labor reports that stock clerks earned a median hourly wage of $9.66 in 2005. Based on a 40-hour workweek, this is an annual salary of $20,100. Experienced stock clerks can earn anywhere from $26,030 to more than $33,760, with time-and-a-half pay for overtime. Those working for large companies or national chains may receive excellent benefits. After one year of employment, some stock clerks are offered one to two weeks of paid vacation each year, as well as health and medical insurance and a retirement plan.

WORK ENVIRONMENT

Stock clerks usually work in relatively clean, comfortable areas. Working conditions vary considerably, however, depending on the industry and the type of merchandise being handled. For example, stock clerks who handle refrigerated goods must spend some time in cold storage rooms, while those who handle construction materials such as bricks and lumber occasionally work outside in harsh weather. Most stock clerk jobs involve much standing, bending, walking, stretching, lifting, and carrying. Some workers may be required to operate machinery to lift and move stock.

Because stock clerks are employed in so many different types of industries, the number of hours worked every week depends on the type of employer. Stock clerks in retail stores usually work a five-day, 40-hour week, while those in industry work 44 hours, or five-and-one-half days, a week. Many others are able to find part-time work. Overtime is common, especially when large shipments arrive or during peak times such as holiday seasons.

OUTLOOK

Although the volume of inventory transactions is expected to increase significantly, employment for stock clerks is expected to decline through 2014, according to the U.S. Department of Labor. This is a result of increased automation and other productivity improvements that enable clerks to handle more stock. Sales-floor stock clerks in grocery, general merchandise, department, apparel, and accessories stores will probably be less affected by automation, as most of their work is difficult to automate.

Because this occupation employs a large number of workers, many job openings will occur each year to replace stock clerks who transfer to other jobs and leave the labor force. Stock clerk jobs tend to be entry-level positions, so many vacancies will be created by normal career progression to other occupations.

FOR MORE INFORMATION

For materials on educational programs in the retail industry, contact
National Retail Federation
325 7th Street NW, Suite 1100
Washington, DC 20004-2818
Tel: 800-673-4692
http://www.nrf.com

Supermarket Workers

OVERVIEW

Supermarket workers are a diverse group. Each supermarket worker is employed in one or more areas of a grocery store, from the checkout lane to the deli counter to the back stock room. There are 3.4 million people who work as employees of food stores, according to the Food Marketing Institute. Supermarkets are located in cities and towns across the nation and include large chains and locally owned stores.

HISTORY

Grocery stores have existed in the United States since the 1800s. Those early stores did not carry a wide variety of merchandise and brands. Many specialized in one area such as bread, fish, or meat. Even these early stores needed workers to help run their businesses. At the time, workers were less specialized; often, the same person who helped wrap the meat at a butcher shop might be found later in the day sweeping out the store.

In the early 1900s, small "mom and pop" stores opened. These stores were the beginning of the modern grocery industry. Soon, some of the stores expanded into chains, and the role of the supermarket worker became even more important. With bigger stores, more merchandise, and more customers, more people were needed to work in the stores.

While technology has eliminated positions in other industries, the grocery industry has wisely utilized technology (such as the bar code system) but has not seen a need to reduce staff. While

QUICK FACTS

School Subjects
Business
English
Mathematics

Personal Skills
Communication/ideas
Following instructions

Work Environment
Primarily indoors
Primarily one location

Minimum Education Level
High school diploma
(or enrolled in high school)

Salary Range
$10,712 to $17,264 to
$28,330+

Certification or Licensing
Required for certain
positions

Outlook
More slowly than the
average

DOT
299

GOE
05.09.01

NOC
6211, 6251, 6611, 6622

O*NET-SOC
N/A

the technology has made efficiency and customer service better, people are still needed to do most of the jobs in a grocery store. One technological change on the horizon is online grocery stores. This is a very new trend, but even online ordering involves order takers, delivery personnel, stock room personnel, inventory control, and more.

THE JOB

There are so many different types of work to do in a grocery that each job can be very different from the next. One of the first positions most people think of in a grocery is the *cashier*. Cashiers are a store's front line for customer service, since they interact with customers all day and ensure order accuracy. Cashiers greet customers, scan merchandise, record coupons, present totals, take payments, and help to bag groceries. It is each cashier's responsibility to keep his or her work area clean and to ensure that the cash drawer balances at the end of his or her shift. If merchandise is marked incorrectly or damaged, the cashier calls the appropriate department to assist the customer.

Along with the cashiers, *clerks* help to bag the groceries; if necessary, they help the customers transport the grocery bags to their vehicles. *Courtesy clerks,* sometimes called *bag boys* or *baggers,* also collect carts from the parking lots and help provide maintenance for those carts.

Stock personnel play an important behind-the-scenes role in supermarkets. They help unload trucks, inspect merchandise, stock shelves, and track inventory. If you visit a grocery late at night, you can see these workers busily preparing for the next day's customers.

Specialization is an important trend in the grocery industry. Since the industry is very competitive, stores are adding more services and conveniences to attract and keep customers. Some of the specialized departments have historically been a part of grocery stores, such as bakeries and meat markets, while others, such as restaurants and baby-sitting services, are new.

Each area requires workers with specialized knowledge and training as well as experience in the grocery industry. Butchers, bakers, and deli workers are generally dedicated to their individual departments in the store, while other workers may "float" to the areas where they are needed.

Other supermarket workers are responsible for certain areas such as produce or dairy. While there is no preparation work involved such as there is in the bakery or deli departments, these workers regularly inspect merchandise, check expiration dates, and maintain displays.

Many supermarkets now include restaurants or food courts that require food preparers, servers, wait staff, and chefs.

Many larger chain supermarkets have a pharmacy on site. *Pharmacists* fill prescriptions for customers and offer counseling on both prescription and over-the-counter medications. *Pharmacy technicians* assist the pharmacist by filling prescriptions, taking inventory, and handling the cash register.

There are also many specialized support positions in supermarkets. *Store detectives* assist with security measures and loss prevention. *Human resource workers* handle personnel-related issues such as recruiting and training, benefits administration, labor relations, and salary administration. These are very important members of the supermarket team, since the average large grocery store employs 250 people. Supermarkets also require qualified accounting and finance workers, advertising workers, marketing workers, information technology professionals, and community and public relations professionals.

Supermarket workers report to either a department or store manager. *Supermarket managers* have to attend weekly departmental meetings and must communicate well with their management, which is usually at the district level. Because many supermarket workers deal directly with customers, their managers depend on them to relay information about customer needs, wants, and dissatisfactions.

According to the U.S. Department of Labor, 31 percent of supermarket workers work part time. For workers with school, family, or other employment, hours are scheduled at the time workers are available, such as evenings and weekends. Since many grocery stores are open 24 hours a day, employees may work during the day or evening hours. Weekend hours are also important, and most grocery stores are open on holidays as well.

All of the different jobs of a supermarket worker have one very important thing in common: They are customer driven. Grocery sales nationwide continue to climb, and customer service is highly important in the grocery business as in all retail businesses.

With that in mind, the primary responsibility of all supermarket workers is to serve the customer. Many secondary duties, such as keeping work areas clean, collecting carts from the parking lot, and checking produce for freshness, are also driven by this main priority.

Supermarket workers arrange a cheese display. *(Ken Hammond, U.S. Dept. of Agriculture)*

REQUIREMENTS

High School

Many workers in the supermarket industry are recent high school graduates or present high school students. There is a large turnover in the field, as many workers move on to other industries. In high school, you should take English, mathematics, business, and computer science classes to learn the basic skills to do most supermarket jobs.

Postsecondary Training

Postsecondary training is not required in the supermarket industry but may be encouraged for specific areas such as the bakery or for management positions. Stores offer on-the-job training and value employees who are able to learn quickly while they work.

Certification or Licensing

To protect the public's health, bakers, deli workers, and butchers are required by law in most states to possess a health certificate and undergo periodic physical exams. These examinations, usually given by the state board of health, make certain that the individual is free from communicable diseases and skin infections.

Other Requirements

The most important requirement for a supermarket worker is the ability to work with people. "With every job I've done here, I've had to help people out," says Nick Williams, who works as a stock boy, bag boy, and cashier at Foods Plus supermarket in Columbus, Indiana. Because workers are required to work with both the public and their own management, communication and customer service skills are important. The ability to follow directions as well as being accurate and honest are qualities that all supermarket workers should possess.

EXPLORING

The best way to find out about what it's like to be a supermarket worker is to become one. Openings for high school students are usually available, and it's a great way to find out about the industry.

Take a class in a supermarket specialty you find interesting. If you think the bakery looks like fun, take a cake-decorating class and find out.

Help out with inventory. Many grocery and retail stores offer limited short-term employment (a day or two a week) for people who can help with inventory during key times of the year. This is a good opportunity to get your foot in the store without making a greater commitment.

Talk to your friends or even your parents. Chances are that they have worked in a grocery store. Find out what they liked and didn't

Did You Know?

- Approximately 3.4 million people are employed in supermarkets.

- There were more than 34,000 supermarkets (with $2 million or more in annual sales) in 2005.

- The average supermarket carries 45,000 items.

- The average supermarket customer spent $27.34 per visit in 2005.

- Sunday is the most popular day for shopping, followed by Saturday and Friday.

Source: Food Marketing Institute

like about the work. Another source for information is your local grocery store. Talk with the people there about their jobs.

EMPLOYERS

There are more than 34,000 supermarkets in the United States, according to the Food Marketing Institute. They are located across the nation, in towns and cities. Some are part of a large chain such as Wal-Mart, Kroger, Albertson's, or Safeway. Other stores are a part of smaller chains or are independently owned.

Workers will have more employment opportunities in cities and large towns where several stores are located. In smaller towns, only one or two stores may serve the area.

STARTING OUT

Nick Williams got his first job in the supermarket in the same way as many others. He applied at the customer service office at the front of the store. Williams was looking for a part-time job with flexible hours and applied at several retail stores in his area.

Besides walk-in applications, groceries use newspaper ads and job drives to attract new employees. Because some of the jobs a supermarket worker may do require little education and pay a modest hourly rate, there are often openings as workers move on to other positions or career fields.

If you apply in person, you should be ready to fill out application materials at the office. Neat dress and good manners are important when applying in person.

Many of today's grocery managers started out as high school clerks or cashiers. It is possible to turn a part-time job into a full-time career. "There are a lot of opportunities to learn different jobs, if you want to," says Williams.

ADVANCEMENT

The opportunities to advance within a supermarket are good if you are dedicated and hard working. With a lot of hard work and dedication, it is possible to advance to a more specialized and better-paying position.

Supermarkets rely heavily on experienced workers, so while a college education might be helpful, it is certainly not required to advance in the field. Relevant experience and hard work are just as beneficial to advancement.

EARNINGS

According to the U.S. Department of Labor, the average nonsupervisory food store employee made $332 per week in 2004. The following are 2005 mean hourly rates for supermarket workers by specialty: cashiers, $8.76; stock clerks and order fillers, $9.86; bakers, $10.84; and butchers and meat cutters, $13.62. Some employees may make less per hour down to the current minimum wage of $5.15 per hour, while more specialized workers in departments may earn more.

Many supermarket workers are part-time employees and do not receive fringe benefits; full-time employees often receive medical benefits and vacation time. Supermarket workers often are eligible for discounts at the stores in which they work, depending on their company policy. The United Food & Commercial Workers International Union represents many supermarket workers concerning pay, benefits, and working-condition issues.

WORK ENVIRONMENT

Some grocery stores are open 24 hours a day, so many workers are required for a variety of shifts. Many supermarket workers are part-time employees and work a varied schedule that changes each week. Depending on the time of day they work, the store may be bustling or quiet. Most of the work is indoors, although some outdoor work may be required to deliver groceries, collect carts, and maintain outside displays. Schedules are usually prepared weekly, and most will include weekend work.

Supermarket workers work in shifts and must work with managers and other workers in a supervisory environment. These managers may be within their department or within the entire store. They must follow directions and report to those managers when required.

OUTLOOK

While the *Career Guide to Industries* (published by the U.S. Department of Labor) predicts only seven percent growth for this industry (as compared to 14 percent for all occupations) through 2014, employment for supermarket workers is good. The field has a large turnover with workers leaving to pursue other careers. Many part-time employees are seasonal and must be replaced often.

As supermarkets add more conveniences for customers, workers will be needed to staff those areas. For example, adding restaurants to supermarkets creates a need for a whole new set of food service workers.

During the past 10 years, the number of grocery stores and supermarkets has declined. Many small chains and local groceries have been purchased by larger chains, and others have gone out of business in the face of the competition.

The U.S. Department of Labor predicts that some occupations in this industry will enjoy stronger growth than the industry average. Bakers, food preparation workers, pharmacists, and pharmacy technicians should enjoy faster-than-average employment growth through 2014.

FOR MORE INFORMATION

For industry and employment information, contact
Food Marketing Institute
655 15th Street NW
Washington, DC 20005-5701
Tel: 202-452-8444
Email: fmi@fmi.org
http://www.fmi.org

For information about the retail industry, contact
National Retail Federation
325 7th Street NW, Suite 1100
Washington, DC 20004-2818
Tel: 202-783-7971
http://www.nrf.com

For information about internships, contact
Retail Industry Leaders Association
1700 North Moore Street, Suite 2250
Arlington, VA 22209-1933
Tel: 703-841-2300
http://www.retail-leaders.org

For information about union membership in the food industry, contact
United Food & Commercial Workers International Union
AFL-CIO/CLC
1775 K Street NW
Washington, DC 20006-1502
Tel: 202-223-3111
http://www.ufcw.org

Wireless Sales Workers

OVERVIEW

Wireless sales workers, also known as *wireless* or *cellular sales representatives*, work for wireless telecommunications service providers to sell products and services to individuals and businesses. The products and services they sell include cellular phones, phone service, pagers, paging service, and various wireless service package options. *Inside sales workers* work on-site at their employers' sales offices, helping customers who come in to inquire about wireless service. *Outside sales workers* travel to call on various potential customers at their offices.

HISTORY

Although you may think of cellular phones as a product of late twentieth century technology, they actually have their beginnings all the way back in the late 1800s. In 1895, an Italian electrical engineer and inventor named Guglielmo Marconi figured out how to transmit signals from one place to another using electromagnetic waves, creating the first radio. One of Marconi's first major successes came in 1896, when he was able to send signals over a distance of more than a mile. Marconi continued to improve and refine his invention. In 1897, he transmitted signals from shore to a ship at sea 18 miles away, and in 1901, he sent signals a distance of 200 miles. By 1905, many ships were regularly using Marconi's radio to communicate with the shore.

QUICK FACTS

School Subjects
Business
Speech

Personal Skills
Communication/ideas

Work Environment
Primarily indoors
One location with some
    travel

Minimum Education Level
High school diploma

Salary Range
$35,000 to $68,000 to
    $110,000

Certification or Licensing
None available

Outlook
Faster than the average

DOT
N/A

GOE
N/A

NOC
0131

O*NET-SOC
41-3099.99

Radio evolved rapidly. By the mid-1920s, more than 1,400 radio stations were broadcasting programming all across America, and by the end of the 1940s, that number had grown to 2,020. Immediately following World War II, radio saw a period of especially rapid development and improvement. Sophisticated transmitting and receiving equipment played a key role in the exploration of space, and in 1969, astronauts on the Apollo mission used a very high-frequency radio communication system to transmit their voices from the Moon back to Earth for the first time.

Cellular radio, which is essentially today's cellular phone service, was first tested in the United States in the 1970s. This system, a miniature version of large radio networks, was named *cellular* because its broadcast area is divided into units called cells. Each cell was equipped with its own radio transmitter, with a range of about 1 to 2.5 miles. As a mobile *radiophone* moved through this network of cells, its calls were switched from one cell to another by a computerized system. It was possible to make calls only within the area covered by the network of cells, however; once the radiophone was outside the cellular area, the connection was lost. First tested in Chicago and the Washington, D.C., area, this cellular system was soon duplicated in other towns, both large and small, throughout the United States. As more and more of the United States became covered with these networks of cells, it became possible to use cellular phones in more places and use of these phones became increasingly widespread.

In order to use a cellular phone, one had to have two things: the phone itself and a subscription to a cellular service. Cellular service providers, much like traditional phone companies, signed users up for phone service to be billed on a monthly basis. Often, as part of the sign-up agreement, the new customer received a free or inexpensive cellular phone. As the availability of cellular service has expanded geographically, the number of people signing up for this service has increased dramatically. According to CTIA-The Wireless Association, in 2006 more than 219 million Americans were wireless service subscribers. Cellular, or wireless, sales workers in communities across the United States have been the liaison between the cellular providers and the cellular users. They have been the workers selling the service, explaining its workings, and signing up new users.

THE JOB

Wireless sales workers sell communications systems, equipment, and services to both businesses and individuals. The products they sell may be divided up into "hard" products—such as pagers or cellular phones—and "soft" products, such as cellular phone service, paging service, voice mail, or phone service options. Most wireless sales workers work for a cellular service provider, trying to persuade prospective buyers to sign up for that provider's phone service. In areas covered by two or more cellular providers, the salesperson may have to convince customers to use his or her provider instead of the competition. In other cases, it is merely a matter of convincing the customer that he or she needs cellular service, explaining what the service provides, and doing the paperwork to begin a contract.

There are two categories of wireless sales workers. Outside sales workers visit prospective clients at their offices. These workers may make appointments in advance, or they may drop in unannounced and ask for a few minutes of the prospective customer's time. This practice is called cold calling. Outside sales workers often call on customers only within a specific geographic territory that may be defined by their employers. Members of the second category, inside sales workers, work in a cellular provider's offices, frequently in a customer showroom. These workers greet and help customers who come into the office to buy or inquire about wireless services. Brian Quigley is the inside sales manager for a major cellular service provider in Bloomington, Indiana. Before becoming the manager, he worked as a sales representative for four years.

There are several aspects of a wireless sales representative's job. The first is generating new customers. Sales workers develop lists of possible customers in many different ways. They may ask for referrals from existing customers, call on new businesses or individuals as they move into their assigned territory, or compile names and numbers from business directories or phone books. They may also attend business trade shows or expositions, or join networking groups where they can make contact with people who might be interested in signing up for their service. Once sales workers have their list of possible contacts, they may send out letters or sales brochures, often following up with a phone call and a request for an appointment.

The second aspect of the job is perhaps the most important. This involves talking with prospective customers about the company's services and products and helping them choose the ones that they will be happy with. In order to do this, the sales worker must have a thorough knowledge of all the company's offerings and be able to explain how these offerings can meet the customer's needs. "We spend a lot of time each day taking sales calls from people or working with walk-ins," Quigley says. "And dealing with people who are considering buying wireless is not a quick process. On the average, you spend between 15 and 30 minutes with one customer, answering all of his or her questions." Answering these questions may involve demonstrating the features of different phones or pagers, going over the pricing structures of various service plans, or explaining how the wireless service works and what its geographic limitations are. The sales worker must try to overcome any objections the customer might have about the products or services and convince him or her to make the purchase. If the salesperson fails to "close the deal" on the first visit, he or she might follow up with more visits, phone calls, or letters.

A wireless sales worker's job usually involves a certain amount of paperwork. When a salesperson makes a sale, he or she may input the customer's billing and credit information into a computer in order to generate a contract, explain the contract to the customer, and ask him or her to sign it. He or she may also do the paperwork necessary to activate the new customer's phone or pager. Sales workers may also maintain records on all their customers, usually in a computer database.

Many sales workers maintain contact with their customers even after making a sale. The salesperson may make a follow-up call to ensure that the customer's service or product is working properly and that he or she is satisfied. The salesperson may also check back periodically to see if the customer is interested in purchasing "upgrades"—new or improved services or products. The sales reps in Quigley's location also help existing customers who have questions about their equipment, service, or billing statement. "You'd be surprised how much of my job is servicing existing customers," he says. "I'll bet I spend 80 percent of my time on customer retention."

Because wireless technology changes so rapidly, learning about new products and services is an important part of a wireless sales worker's job. He or she may frequently attend seminars or training programs to keep current on the latest in wireless products, in order to be able to explain them to potential customers. Quigley says that his company holds quarterly sales rallies, where wireless equipment manufacturers come to explain and demonstrate their new products. "A lot of the stuff you just have to learn on your own, too," he says. "Because things change so rapidly, you often can't wait until the next sales rally to find out about a piece of equipment. You just have to crack open the manual and read up on it."

REQUIREMENTS

High School

The minimum educational level needed to become a wireless sales worker is a high school diploma. To prepare for a career in wireless sales, you should choose high school classes that will help you understand and communicate with people. Courses in speech, English, and psychology are all good options for this. You might also want to take classes that help you understand basic business principles, such as business and math courses. Finally, it may be helpful to take some fundamental computer classes in order to become familiar with keyboarding and using some basic software applications. Like virtually all other offices, wireless offices are typically computerized—so you will probably need to be comfortable operating a computer.

Postsecondary Training

Although there are no formal requirements, it is becoming more and more common for wireless sales workers to have a two- or four-year college degree. Brian Quigley began his career in wireless sales after obtaining a bachelor's degree in marketing, and he says that his company prefers to recruit college graduates. Many employers consider a bachelor's degree in marketing, business, or telecommunications to be especially beneficial. In addition, because wireless services are so heavily dependent on technology, some wireless sales workers enter the field with a technology-related degree.

Whether a new wireless sales worker has a college degree or not, there are likely to be aspects of the job and the company that he or she is not familiar with. Therefore, most wireless service companies provide training programs for their newly hired workers. These programs, which may last from three weeks to three months, cover such topics as cellular technologies, product lines, sales techniques, using the company's computer system, entering orders, and other company policies.

Other Requirements

Successful wireless sales workers have a combination of personal characteristics that allow them to do their jobs well. Perhaps the most important is the ability to connect and communicate with people; without this quality, it is virtually impossible to be an effective salesperson. Wireless salespersons should enjoy interacting with people, feel comfortable talking with people they do not know, and be able to communicate clearly and persuasively. "You also have to be a good listener, in addition to a good talker," Quigley says. "When someone is upset, you have to hear what they are saying and be able to appease them." The ability to work in a high-pressure, competitive environment is also an important characteristic. Many wireless sales workers earn the majority of their income from commissions or bonuses. In addition, most workers are expected to meet monthly or quarterly sales goals set by the company. Successful sales workers should be able to handle the stress of working to meet these goals. Self-confidence is another essential quality of good sales workers. Any sales job will involve a certain amount of rejection from customers who are not interested or not ready to buy. Salespersons must be secure and confident enough to avoid letting this rejection affect them on a personal level. According to Quigley, the willingness to learn and change is also highly important to success in this field. "This industry is always changing, sometimes so quickly that it's hard to keep up with it," he says. "You have to be prepared for the changes."

EXPLORING

You can find out what it is like to be a wireless sales worker by visiting the offices of a local cellular provider. By talking with the sales staff and perhaps observing them as they work, you should be able to get a feel for what the day-to-day job entails. One of the best ways to find out firsthand if you enjoy selling is to find a summer or after-school job in sales. To learn more about wireless technology and the products available, visit your local library and see what books and magazine articles are available—or do some online research, if you have access to the Internet.

EMPLOYERS

Most of the major telecommunications companies throughout the United States offer wireless service in addition to their traditional phone service. For example, AT&T, Sprint, MCI, and Verizon all have wireless divisions—and, consequently, wireless sales staff. There are also many smaller wireless providers, such as U.S. Cellular, Nextel Partners, and others. Each of these smaller providers also has a sales staff, although in many cases a much smaller one. These providers are located throughout the United States, in virtually every medium-sized and large community. You should be able to find a list of them by asking your local librarian for help or by doing a keyword search on "wireless service providers" on the Internet.

STARTING OUT

To find a job in wireless sales, you should first determine which wireless service providers operate in your area. Check directly with these providers to find out if they have any openings, or send them a resume and cover letter. If you are willing to relocate, you might contact the national headquarters of each of the large wireless companies mentioned earlier to find out what jobs are available nationwide. Many of these companies even have Web sites that list current job openings. You might also keep an eye on local or regional newspapers. Telecommunications companies, including wireless providers, frequently post job openings in the classified sections of these newspapers. If you have attended a college or university, check with your school's career services office to see if it has any contacts with wireless service providers.

Many wireless providers prefer to hire applicants with proven sales records. This may be especially true in cases where the applicant has only a high school degree. If you find that you are having difficulty obtaining a position in wireless sales, you might consider first taking another sales job (perhaps in electronic or communications equipment) to gain experience. Once you have proven your abilities, you may have better luck being hired for a wireless sales position.

ADVANCEMENT

For most wireless salespersons, advancement comes in the form of increased income via commissions and bonuses. A proven sales worker might earn the title of *senior sales representative* or *senior account executive*. These workers may be given better territories or larger, more important accounts to handle. Some sales workers eventually move into managerial roles as they expand in their capabilities and knowledge of the company. A sales worker might move into the position of *sales manager,* for example. In this position, he or she would oversee other salespersons, either for the entire organization or for a specific geographic territory. Brian Quigley became the sales manager for his location after four years of working as a sales representative. The next step on the career ladder for him is *general manager* of retail stores, which would put him in charge of a specific geographic region. Another advancement possibility in larger companies is that of trainer. In the role of *sales trainer,* a sales worker would be responsible for developing, coordinating, and training new employees in sales techniques.

EARNINGS

For motivated and skilled salespersons, the pay for wireless sales can be quite good. Most companies offer their sales staff a small base salary and incentive pay in the form of commissions, bonuses, or both. In some cases, the incentive pay can increase the salesperson's base salary by up to 75 percent. Because most salespersons earn the majority of their income through incentive pay, the income level depends greatly upon individual performance.

According to the *U.S. News & World Report's* "Best Jobs for the Future," the average beginning wireless sales worker might expect to earn around $35,000. A senior sales worker might earn around $68,000, and a top sales executive can make as much as $110,000. Wireless sales managers can expect to earn between $75,000 and $80,000.

Sales workers employed by most wireless companies receive a benefits package, which typically includes health insurance and paid vacation, sick days, and holidays. Outside sales workers may be provided with a company car and an expense account to pay for food, lodging, and travel expenses incurred while traveling on company business.

WORK ENVIRONMENT

Inside sales representatives typically work in comfortable, attractively decorated customer showrooms. They usually have desks either in the showroom or in a back office, where they can do their paperwork and perhaps meet with customers. While many sales reps work regular 40-hour weeks, Monday through Friday, it is not at all uncommon for these workers to work longer-than-average weeks. In addition, many wireless sales offices are open on weekends to accommodate customers who cannot come in during the week. Therefore, some sales workers spend weekend hours at the office.

Outside sales workers may spend much of their time traveling to meet on-site with various potential customers. Unless a salesperson's territory is very large, however, overnight travel is uncommon. When not traveling, outside sales workers may spend time in the office, setting up appointments with customers, keeping records, and completing paperwork. Both types of sales workers spend the majority of their time dealing with people. In addition to customer contact, these salespersons often work cooperatively with service technicians and customer service staff.

OUTLOOK

Job opportunities for wireless sales workers are expected to grow at a rate faster than the average. CTIA-The Wireless Association reports that more than 72 percent of the U.S. population now has a wireless phone. Part of the reason for this growth is that technological advances are making wireless phones and pagers more effective and useful all the time. One of the most recent developments, digital communication technology, is especially expected to increase wireless phone use by offering better quality and range. Wireless service is also being increasingly used to transmit data as well as voice. Examples of wireless data communication include such applications as faxing, email, games, media downloads, and Internet access. In addition, new technology, widespread use of wireless services, and more leverage for the consumer as a result of federal legislation (such as being able to change providers and keeping the same wireless phone number) have driven the prices of service down. This means that wireless services are now an option for many people who previously couldn't afford them. All of these factors combined should spur the need for a growing number of sales workers. The demand for jobs will also be enhanced by the high turnover in the sales field as a whole. Each year, many sales workers leave their jobs—in wireless and other industries—because they fail to make enough money or feel they are not well suited to the demanding career. New sales workers must then be hired to replace those who have left the field.

FOR MORE INFORMATION

For job postings, links to wireless industry recruiters, industry news, and training information, contact or visit the following Web site
CTIA-The Wireless Association
1400 16th Street NW, Suite 600
Washington, DC 20036-2225
Tel: 202-785-0081
http://www.ctia.org

For the latest on the wireless industry, contact
Wireless Industry Association
8290 West Sahara Avenue, Suite 160
Las Vegas, NV 89117-8931
Tel: 800-624-6918
http://wirelessdealers.com

For a brochure on mobile phone etiquette and other information on the wireless industry in Canada, contact or visit the following Web site

Canadian Wireless Telecommunications Association
130 Albert Street, Suite 1110
Ottawa, ON K1P 5G4
Canada
Tel: 613-233-4888
Email: info@cwta.ca
http://www.cwta.ca

Index